Soldiers Blue

SOLDIERS BLUE

~

How Bomber Command and Area Bombing Helped Win the Second World War

by David L. Bashow

CANADIAN DEFENCE ACADEMY PRESS

Canadian Defence Academy Press
PO Box 17000 Stn Forces
Kingston, Ontario   K7K 7B4

Produced for the Canadian Defence Academy Press
by 17 Wing Winnipeg Publishing Office.
WPO30669

FRONT COVER: *Girl from the North Country*. A Lancaster Mk. X from 431 Iroquois Squadron unloads a graffiti-rich 4000 pound 'cookie' on Germany while a German night fighter overshoots. The nose art on *She's Truly Terrific*, Lancaster KB811, coded SE-T, was inspired by the popular pin-up artist, Alberto Vargas. CREDIT: Painting by Patricia McNorgan.

BACK COVER CREDIT: Library and Archives Canada (LAC) PC2475.

Library and Archives Canada Cataloguing in Publication

Bashow, David L., 1946-
Soldiers blue : how bomber command and area bombing helped win the Second World War / by David L. Bashow.

Produced for the Canadian Defence Academy Press by 17 Wing Winnipeg Publishing Office.
Includes bibliographical references and index.
Available also on the Internet.
Issued by: Canadian Defence Academy.
ISBN 978-1-100-18028-1
Cat. no.: D2-273/2011E

1. World War, 1939-1945--Aerial operations, British. 2. Bombing, Aerial--Germany--History. 3. Great Britain. Royal Air Force. Bomber Command. 4. World War, 1939-1945--Destruction and pillage--Germany. 5. World War, 1939-1945--Aerial operations, American. 6. World War, 1939-1945--Campaigns--Western Front. I. Canadian Defence Academy II. Canada. Canadian Armed Forces. Wing, 17 III. Title. IV. Title: How bomber command and area bombing helped win the Second World War.

D785 B37 2011   940.54'4941   C2011-980029-2

ACKNOWLEDGEMENTS

Soldiers Blue is truly a collective effort. With that in mind, I wish to express my sincere appreciation to Colonel Bernd Horn and Dr. Bill Bentley of the CDA Press and the Canadian Forces Leadership Institute respectively for giving me the opportunity to provide some positive balance to what I believe has become a widespread ignorance and lack of appreciation of a formidable contribution to victory for the Allied cause during the Second World War.

Within the Canadian Defence Academy Headquarters, I am particularly grateful to Mr. Craig Mantle for his boundless enthusiasm and 'can do' spirit in helping me to obtain the many visual elements needed to supplement the written word. Similar kudos to Mélanie Denis for her cheerful support and unending patience in keeping me focused and on track.

Finally, I would like to thank Patricia McNorgan for her gracious permission to use her evocative *Girl from the North Country* on the cover of this book. I believe this combat depiction truly captures the essence of the Bomber Command contribution.

David L. Bashow
Kingston, Ontario

CREDIT: Courtesy of Halifax Restoration Project Trenton.

A Canadian *Halifax* crew in a happy wartime moment.

FOREWORD

I am very pleased to introduce Lieutenant-Colonel (ret'd) David Bashow's latest contribution to the historical debate with respect to the contributions of wartime Bomber Command to Allied victory during the Second World War. The author has already written much on this subject, providing fresh looks at the bombing campaign by emphasizing the highly significant role it played in defeating the Axis powers. In brief, the Allied bombardment of the Third Reich and its allies was part and parcel of Britain's overall war strategy to carry the fight to the enemy, particularly during the early war years, when no other significant form of sustained offensive action was viable.

DAVID L. BASHOW

The *direct* benefits to victory brought about by the bombing have long been trivialized by its detractors, but the *indirect* effects of the bombing are perhaps of even greater importance. After the summer of 1941, assuaging the Soviet allies, it created a 'poor man's second front' that bled off resources from Germany's Eastern campaign, diverting massive amounts of materiel and manpower to address the bombing threat, and the damage that it meted out.

In an even broader sense, the bombing dealt telling blows to Germany's economic and industrial infrastructure, forcing the *decentralization* of its war industries upon an industrial society that had been deliberately *centralized* for maximum efficiency. This dispersal of effort, in turn, placed incredible additional strains and burdens upon a transportation network that was already taxed to the limit. In the final analysis, along with significant destruction/disruption of the enemy's war industries, it helped pave the way, through assisting in the destruction of the enemy's air defences, oil resources, and its extensive and varied transportation networks, for a successful invasion of the Third Reich through northwest Europe in 1944.

One of many German industrial centres left in ruins from the bombing.

CREDIT: Library and Archives Canada (LAC) PL52655.

DAVID L. BASHOW

Bashow dispels the "myths" of American "precision" bombardment versus British "area" bombing, and that the bomber offensive was misdirected use of scant resources, having limited effect on the war effort. He also argues that Bomber Command's counter-oil and transportation campaigns were much more effective than the detractors have acknowledged, and that this effort played a great part in the attainment of Allied air superiority. Finally, the application of the European experience of area bombing played a significant role in bringing the war in the Pacific against the Japanese to a decisive and much less costly conclusion than that which would have been accomplished by a successful Allied invasion of the Japanese Home Islands, were that option even possible.

I highly commend *Soldiers Blue* to all those who wish to further their education and appreciation of the results obtained by the Allied Combined Bomber Offensive against the Axis powers during the Second World War.

Major-General J.P.Y.D. Gosselin, CMM, CD
Commander
Canadian Defence Academy

A late-war Canadian *Halifax* crew from 434 *Bluenose* Squadron, Royal Canadian Air Force.

TABLE OF CONTENTS

An Avro *Lancaster*, perhaps the aircraft most symbolic of Bomber Command's war.

Introduction

During the autumn of 2008, I was saddened to see the controversy associated with the Second World War's Allied Combined Bomber Offensive (CBO) against the Axis powers fanned up again in Randall Hansen's *Fire and Fury ~ The Allied Bombing of Germany 1942-45*. In my opinion, Professor Hansen uses visceral triggers, the undeniable carnage embodied in the human cost of the Allied bombing campaign, and couples them with hyperbole and inappropriate generalizations to sensationalize this strategic direction. He also uses isolated uncharacteristic quotations from principal characters in this complex train of events to advance his case that the bomber offensive, particularly as it was conducted by Britain's Bomber Command, was both immoral and ineffective. And while I respect and support his right and those of other prominent detractors of the campaign to voice their views, I submit they cannot be allowed to go unchallenged. Specifically, Professor Hansen alleges that:

- The bomber offensive was a waste of scarce wartime resources that could have been utilized more effectively when applied to other combat initiatives;

- The area bombing of the Axis industrial centres probably prolonged rather than shortened the war, and that it had no measurable, substantive effect upon war production;

- The deliberate area bombing of enemy civilians, if not illegal, was certainly immoral, and that much of the city bombing simply constituted acts of wanton destruction, that they were generated primarily to propagate terror, perhaps best exemplified by the February 1945 bombing of Dresden;

- Sir Arthur Harris as Air Officer Commanding-in-Chief (AOC-in-C) of Bomber Command was the senior British air leader most responsible for the strategic concentration upon the area bombing campaign, and that in following this direction, he did not enjoy the approval and support of the Chief of the Air Staff (CAS), Sir Charles Portal;

- The American direction of 'precision' strategic bombing was much more effective, productive, and discriminatory than the area bombing practiced by Bomber Command;

- Bomber Command's campaign against enemy transportation resources was largely ineffective;

- The counter-oil campaign as waged by the Americans was much more effective and timely than that waged by the British; and

- The defeat of the *Luftwaffe* and the concomitant attainment of air superiority in the West were due almost entirely to the 'precision' strategic bombing endeavours of the Americans.

While I intend to address all these specific issues, in the interests of communications brevity, I will only summarize briefly the results obtained by the campaign, and elaborate selectively upon those recently brought to the forefront by Doctor Hansen and other detractors of Bomber Command's wartime strategy. This is because my views on this subject, supported by many primary source and secondary references, have already been published extensively, including a comprehensive analysis of the bombing results in *Canadian Military History*, Vol. 15, Nos. 3 & 4, Autumn 2006, as well as in my previous full-length books on wartime Bomber Command, namely, *No Prouder Place ~ Canadians and the Bomber Command Experience 1939-1945* (2005), and *None but the Brave ~ The Essential Contributions of RAF Bomber Command to Allied Victory during the Second World War* (2009). Nonetheless, I believe that in order for readers to properly appreciate the strategic course adopted by Bomber Command, and since the nub of Professor Hansen's objections centre around the area bombing strategy, a review of the evolution and development of the Command's bombing policy is both necessary and appropriate.

For much of the war, the bomber offensive constituted for Britain and the Dominions the only viable form of offensive action against a thoroughly evil, repressive regime. Lacking a strong continental army, loath to revisit the *abattoir* of massive armies stalemated in bloody confrontation that had characterized the Western Front during the First World War, and realizing that a naval blockade of Germany was impossible in this war, due to the strength of the German navy (*Kriegsmarine*), the bomber offensive became the only viable means of striking back for several years. It provided a massive diversion to the Soviet allies when none other was yet possible, and it constituted the very embodiment of an overall guerrilla warfare strategy, attacking the enemy on its peripheries, in this case, its industrial centres.

The CBO was a highly effective prolonged cooperative effort between the American United States Strategic Air Force (USSTAF) and the

'British' (Bomber Command) camps. Throughout the campaign, while both camps at times placed the emphasis of efforts upon different components of the enemy's war-making capabilities, there was a tremendous amount of overall synergism and mutual support. For example, the combined efforts of Bomber Command and the USSTAF ultimately destroyed virtually all of Germany's coke, ferroalloy, and synthetic rubber industries, 95 percent of its fuel, hard coal, and rubber capacity, and 90 percent of its steel capacity.[1]

Conversely, Bomber Command attacked many precision manufacturing targets during the course of the war.

CREDIT: LAC PL10811.

Heading to war, and boarding the crew bus.

The Evolution of a Hurricane

There is no doubt that British bombing policy, as it was conducted during the Second World War, was influenced by the strategic aerial bombardment experiences of the First World War. German airship

(*Zeppelin*) and giant fixed-wing bomber raids on Britain produced nearly 3500 fatal casualties and left many others injured. Moreover, these raids generated widespread shock, a sense of vulnerability, and a significant disruption of wartime production all out of proportion to the actual damage they inflicted. This included lost time due to the suspension of manufacturing, the upheaval of transportation systems, worker consternation and anxiety, and the diversion of limited human and materiel resources to directly combat these threats.[2] A postwar bombing survey concluded that although the *material* damage had been light, panic had been widespread in the cities attacked. Attempting to foresee the future efficacy of aerial bombardment, and based upon the bombing results observed in both Britain and Germany, the Chief of the Air Staff, Sir Hugh (later Viscount) Trenchard felt that material damage to the enemy would be very secondary compared to the chaos sown by the *moral(e)*[sic] *collapse* of personnel working in the vital public services sectors, such as water supply, food services distribution, lighting, power, and transportation.[3] Thus, throughout the 1920s and early 1930s, Trenchard, in lockstep with parallel doctrine espoused by the Italian general Guilio Douhet and the American general "Billy" Mitchell, essentially helped shape the Royal Air Force's (RAF) conventional wisdom that "...the bomber would always get through," and that determined aerial attacks upon an enemy's war economy "...would produce such crushing damage to both natural resources and civilian morale that the opponent would have to sue for peace."[4]

CREDIT: RAF photo.

One of the earliest of Bomber Command's wartime steeds, a Bristol *Blenheim*, in a steep turn.

When Bomber Command was officially established in 1936, the RAF War Manual clearly stated, "…the bomb is the chief weapon of an air force."[5] And the new Command was formed within a parent service that had been seamlessly committed to the utility of a strategic bombing policy from that service's conception. Further, the perception of the relative invulnerability of the bomber had been erroneously reinforced through acts of indiscriminate area bombardment of civilians during the inter-war years by various totalitarian nations, including the Japanese upon defenceless Chinese ports, the Italians upon native villages in Abyssinia, and, perhaps most notably, by the fascists under Spanish Generalissimo Francisco Franco upon Barcelona, then Guernica, in April 1937. These bombings served chilling notice to the western democracies of a distinct lack of scruples associated with the use of this weapon by the totalitarian regimes; a realization that would be strongly reinforced by the indiscriminate application of area bombing by the Germans against civilians during the early months of the Second World War. In fairness, these perceptions were also reinforced by various bombing sorties conducted by the British in the Middle East during the 'police actions' of the inter-war years.

Just prior to the 1938 Munich Crisis, Bomber Command's AOC-in-C, Air Marshal Sir Edgar Ludlow-Hewitt, told Prime Minister (PM) Neville Chamberlain that Bomber Command was virtually useless in its present state. He asserted that his aircraft could only reach the peripheries of northwestern Germany, and that they would incur unacceptably high combat losses against known German defences. Further, he maintained that to commit the Command to offensive action in its present state would be courting disaster. Even as late as the spring of 1940, when the German *Blitzkrieg* rolled through France and the Low Countries, the Command was essentially confined to assisting the land battle on the continent, possessing still nothing but the most rudimentary attack capabilities.

However, policy-makers made it clear that unrestricted bombardment was not considered to be in the interests of Great Britain in 1938. And the ban on posing a risk to civilian lives would only be lifted in May 1940, and then, somewhat tentatively, when Winston Churchill replaced Neville Chamberlain as prime minister, and after the indiscriminate early-war bombings of Warsaw, Rotterdam, and other urban centres by the Germans.

CREDIT: LAC PL4958.

An early-war shot of a navigator at his station.

To War

Thus, British bombing policy was deliberately non-provocative at the commencement of hostilities in 1939, restricted to daylight reconnaissance, leaflet raids, and attacks upon enemy shipping and ports. But Bomber Command's daylight raids soon resulted in decimation of the attacking forces, and a policy shift to night attacks in an attempt to use the cloak of darkness for compensatory protection. Notwithstanding, night attacks were fraught with difficulties and challenges. And while daylight, precision raids had become prohibitively dangerous, astral-navigation could, at best, get the crews to within twelve miles of a specific target. Nor were electronic navigational beacons, still relatively new and limited, expected to make much of a difference for night attacks.

Looking to the future, but persuaded that Bomber Command required additional time to build up its strength, the air staff now began to argue that the focus of bombing should shift from producing physical damage…, to lowering enemy morale, which it wishfully thought could be accomplished by as few as two hundred sorties a week. The idea was to dispatch small numbers of aircraft to Germany each night, dispersing them in time and space through as many air defence zones as possible and setting off almost continuous alarms over the whole Reich. This would upset the "nerves and digestion" of the German population and might eventually make living conditions so unpleasant that those employed in the war industries would be "…loath to continue at work."[6]

Nonetheless, decisive results were not expected from this psychological approach. In order to inflict significant damage, intelligence staff felt the Axis oil industry needed targeting, and concluded that the neutralization of 22 of Germany's facilities, of which 15 were located less than 150 miles from the North Sea, could have a decisive impact upon the German war effort. Thus, on 22 February 1940, the RAF CAS, Sir Cyril Newall, approved an oil plan just when Bomber Command began its full conversion to a night bombing force.[7] Nonetheless, Air Marshal Charles Portal, Bomber Command's new helmsman (having recently replaced Ludlow-Hewitt in a normal progression), was not sanguine, and he told Newall that target identification at night, for average crews, was only possible under the best conditions of visibility, and then, only when the target was on the coast or an enormous waterway, such as the Rhine River. Beyond this, very few inexperienced crews "…could be likely to find it under any condition."[8]

CREDIT: Imperial War Museum (IWM) TR2.

Sir Charles Portal

On 9 April 1940, when the Germans invaded Norway and Denmark, Portal implored his superiors to give his command free rein in an air offensive against civilian morale, but the senior political leadership remained reluctant as long as Britain had not yet been directly bombed. However, on 15 May, after the decimating bombing of Rotterdam the day prior, 'the gloves finally came off,' and Bomber Command was authorized to attack oil refineries and railroad targets west of the Rhine River.[9] At this point, it is important to understand that oil processing facilities tended to be pinpoint targets rather than area targets, and they generally required a high degree of targeting accuracy to assure their destruction.

While intelligence and planning staffs struggled to identify and prioritize the greatest threats and vulnerable enemy areas, including aircraft assembly plants, airfields, and aircraft storage areas, oil, barges, troop ships and ports, over the next few months, no less than six separate bombing policy directives were advanced. Nonetheless, Portal and his staff were not happy with *any* of these directives, and remained convinced that Command crews were simply incapable of finding and destroying precise targets such as oil refineries. They specifically asked for authority to make generalized area attacks against larger German industrial areas in order to undermine enemy morale, having heard through the Foreign Office that the bombing to date was instilling panic among the German population.[10] Portal believed, along with much of the nation's senior civilian and uniformed leadership, that an unfettered campaign against the German industrial cities might impact enemy morale significantly and save the United Kingdom from an invasion. And while Portal's request was summarily denied, the Air Ministry insisting that material destruction still had to be the primary goal at this particular time, it would set the stage for future policy shifts that would alter the fates of many German civilians. Indeed, from 1941 until mid-1944, a significant portion of Bomber Command's sorties consisted of area bombing by night, the chief reason being that "...the only target on which the night force could inflict effective damage was a whole German town."[11] The RAF's Official History Branch Narrative has identified this linkage directly with Sir Charles Portal and the more pessimistic yet pragmatic attitude he brought to future Air Staff deliberations on bombing policy. Portal firmly believed that concentration of air power against the enemy's weakest points would make invasion unnecessary, and he did not hesitate to advise the prime minister accordingly. Ultimately, "... due allowance was made for the inaccuracy of bombing, by ensuring that targets selected were not isolated, but if possible in large centres of population and industry. This was the reason for the initiation of area bombing and the selection of 'industrial centres' instead of factories."[12] This becomes important downstream, since Bomber Command's most famous wartime commander, Sir Arthur 'Bomber' Harris, has been the individual wrongly considered by Professor Hansen most responsible for instituting Bomber Command's area bombing policy, although Harris did execute it earnestly. Conversely, Hansen places great stock in Portal's leadership in directions he maintains were diametrically opposed to those of Harris, an assertion which will be discussed later in some depth.

In terms of policy inputs from senior leadership, as early as 8 July 1940, Churchill had written:

> When I look round to see how we can win the war I see that there is only one sure path. We have no continental army which can defeat the German military power. The blockade is broken and Hitler has Asia and probably Africa to draw from. Should he be repulsed here or not try invasion, he will recoil eastward, and we have nothing to stop him. But there is one thing that will bring him back and bring him down, and that is an absolutely devastating, exterminating attack by very heavy bombers from this country upon the Nazi homeland.[13]

In counterpoint, on 9 October 1940, after repeated attacks upon the British cities, *Reichmarschall* Hermann Göring, Commander-in-Chief of the *Luftwaffe*, made public a plan for the obliteration of London and the demoralization of its citizens by bombardment, coupled with the paralyzing of Britain's broader industrial and commercial capabilities.[14]

Inch by painful inch, both British and German policies were slipping from ones aimed at precise objectives to ones of area bombing with psychological overtones. On 2 September, for example, Portal observed that although he was not yet involved in attempts to burn down whole towns, "that stage will come." The next day Churchill asked that Bomber Command "pulverize the entire industry and economic structure" of the German war economy; and, three days later, he called for a series of "minor" but "widespread" attacks on smaller German towns intended to "destroy the population's faith in their air defences."[15]

CREDIT: Shorts 65133.

A Short *Stirling* heading to war, with a Famous British Person in the foreground.

Shortly thereafter, Portal was elevated to Chief of the Air Staff, and Sir Richard Peirse, a staunch advocate of area bombing, was made AOC-in-C of Bomber Command. Henceforth, Portal's desire to attack the industrial centres as frequently as possible would carry significant weight. And while oil targets carried top priority on clear, moonlit nights when visual target acquisition was at least possible, when it was darker, Bomber Command was "…[to] make a definite attempt… to affect the morale of the German people."[16] An interesting letter of the period, written by Secretary of State for Air Sir Archibald Sinclair to the prime minister, noted that when piecemeal harassment attacks against the German cities were directed at their railway marshalling yards, the results, confirmed by intelligence reports, were encouraging.[17] Such wartime snippets of intelligence, coupled with a certain application of previous British experiences, played a large part in determining broader policies, including bombing priorities.

The results of early city raids proved to be somewhat disappointing, and an over-optimistic report on the damage inflicted to date on enemy synthetic oil refineries, soon dispelled, was also forthcoming. However, Portal conceded the importance of the oil theme, and ordered a campaign against 17 of the Reich's largest synthetic oil plants. The attacks on area targets were to be relegated to nights when weather precluded action against the more demanding, pinpoint refinery targets. For emphasis, Peirse was officially informed on 15 January 1941 that destruction of enemy oil facilities was deemed to be the "sole primary aim" of the bombers until further orders were received.[18] That said, Britain's War Cabinet was not at this time of a mind "…to discourage ruthlessness by Bomber Command; the feeling was that the British people were entitled to know that they were giving as good as they were getting."[19]

On 9 July 1941, yet another policy directive postulated that "…the weakest points in [the enemy's] armour lie in the morale of the civilian population and in his inland transportation system."[20] This directive would pave the way for even broader policy changes, and henceforth, Germany would be bombed more frequently, with greater intensity, and with less target discrimination.

Throughout the first half of 1941, although the Command's operations had continued at a brisk pace whenever weather and opportunity permitted, it was becoming increasingly obvious that the night campaign was not meeting damage expectations. Delivery accuracy was still woefully inadequate. By one report, "… in May 1941 over half the bombs dropped by Bomber Command fell in the country, away from villages, towns and cities."[21] Giving voice to this concern, in August, Frederick Lindemann (later Lord Cherwell), Churchill's chief scientific advisor and trusted confidant, tasked Mr. D.M. Butt of the War Cabinet to examine existing crew bombing results to obtain an accurate picture of actual results. They were sobering. The Butt Report ultimately stressed the need to examine bombing techniques and to improve navigational procedures, the only realistic alternative of massive daylight raids being considered just too dangerous.

However, the War Cabinet concurred that it was unthinkable to abandon the bomber offensive in spite of its shortcomings, since it was, at the time, the only viable way to strike back at the enemy. The report also included an examination of the effect of bombing on civilian morale, based upon British experience during the Blitz, and concluded that bomb damage to homes, water supply, power sources and the food distribution systems had a greater effect on lowering morale than did the loss of friends or relatives. Ultimately, these observations would have an enormous impact on bombing policy.

In sum, the Butt Report deemed pathetic the bombing with respect to accuracy and results obtained for the costs incurred. In the near future, in acknowledgement of existing and anticipated capabilities, less target discrimination would be demanded and more aids to navigation and targeting would be developed by Britain's scientific community. Lord Cherwell, a firm believer in the efficacy of area bombing, and in full agreement with the Butt Report, presented a seminal paper to Cabinet that advocated area bombing as the keystone of a concentrated strategic bombing campaign against the Axis forces. The plan proposed attacking Germany's industrial centres in order to destroy as much working class housing as possible in order to displace the German work force and to disrupt/reduce their ability to work. Although Cherwell's plan was highly controversial from the outset,[22] it was approved by Cabinet, since its members believed that it was the only option available at the time to take the offensive directly to Germany, as Britain was not even remotely ready for a land invasion of the European continent, and because the Soviets were stridently demanding pressure relief from the Western Allies for their Eastern Front.[23]

CREDIT: LAC PL10457.

An early *Halifax* B. Mk. I of 405 Squadron RCAF banks for the camera.

The next pivotal bombing policy direction came on 14 February 1942, with the release of Policy Directive #22. Issued by Portal as CAS, and as a direct result of the Butt Report and Cherwell's approved Cabinet presentation, Portal mandated that henceforth, the primary objective as Bomber Command was to be "... the morale of the enemy civil population, and, in particular, of the industrial workers."[24] These attacks were to be manifested as large raids upon selected area targets in the major industrial areas of Germany, and while industrial, military, and infrastructure aim points were always to be identified and specified, collateral damage in terms of 'dehousing' the civilian population was considered an acceptable, indeed, a *desirable* adjunct to the bombing. The Ruhr area, especially Essen, as well as Berlin, was considered of primary interest. Further, "...to make sure there was no misunderstanding about what was being called for, the next day Portal told his DCAS [Deputy Chief of the Air Staff] to remind High Wycombe [Bomber Command Headquarters] that '...the aiming points are to be the built-up areas, not, for instance, the dockyards or aircraft factories where these are mentioned."[25] This last point deserves emphasis, for it acknowledges the Command's non-precision capabilities at this particular point of the war, and also the generalized propensity in the Western world for building up suburbs around industrial complexes. It is also important to understand that aiming for the hub of an industrial city was likely to inflict damage upon key transportation and communications nodes, such as railway stations and marshalling yards, since they tended to be centralized within urban developments. As summarized by the distinguished American historian Williamson Murray, in keeping with the limited navigation, target identification, target marking, and overall non-precision weapons delivery capabilities of Bomber Command, exacerbated by the realities of industrial dispersal and residential build-up around industrial sites, along with the centralization of many of the major communications and transportation facilities, Bomber Command inexorably "...came to rely upon the dislocation of the German work force rather than the exclusive destruction of the enemy's industrial plants in order to try to achieve its war aims."[26] This is not to imply that all Bomber Command's wartime attacks against the cities were this indiscriminate or standardized. Very frequently, specific industrial, military, and infrastructure aim points were designated and marked, particularly later in the war, when electronic aids, tactics, and weaponry had become further refined. And while it is probably fair to say that urban centres were the default aim point of the Command throughout much of the war, it must be emphasized that the industrial city bombing constituted only a portion of the Command's efforts. To be precise, of Bomber Command's wartime total 955,044 tons of ordnance dropped upon the Third Reich and its proxies, only 430,747 tons (45.1 percent) were dropped upon the industrial cities. The Command was not simply a force dedicated to the assault of Germany's economic system.[27]

CREDIT: IWM CH13020.

Sir Arthur Harris

A New Helmsman

On 24 February 1942, Arthur Harris replaced Sir Richard Peirse as the AOC-in-C of Bomber Command. Throughout the war, Harris would remain hostile to the concept of 'panacea' targets, specific elements of the enemy's military, industrial, and infrastructure capabilities and capacities that, if totally eliminated, would destroy its ability to wage war. And although the accuracy of Bomber Command increased remarkably over the course of the war, Harris believed that an enemy economy and social structure could not be dislocated by an attack on just one of its many elements with the prospect of forcing a political decision to capitulate. Electronic aids, sophisticated marking techniques, stabilized automatic bomb sights, vastly improved weaponry, and highly refined, sophisticated attack tactics would improve significantly delivery accuracies over the course of the war for Bomber Command's

DAVID L. BASHOW

Main Force. However, with the exception of several highly specialized precision attack units, such as 617 and 9 Squadrons flying *Lancasters*, and 106 Squadron of the Light Night Striking Force flying *Mosquitos*, the bulk of the Command remained 'a blunt instrument,' generally incapable of attacking targets with the uncanny precision, accuracy, and reliability of today's forces and munitions. This in mind, Harris pursued a broader strategy that he believed would use that instrument to best affect, and his dogged obstinacy to reject all specific, exclusive types of targets (notably ball bearings, but particularly oil) would become the main objection to his wartime leadership of the Command.[28]

On attacking the enemy work force, Harris believed that bombing out significant numbers of workers meant that vast resources, both materiel and manpower, had to be devoted to their care after the attacks, including repair and reconstruction crews, specialized heavy rescue teams, and special organizations devoted to evacuation and relocation. Collectively, he believed it all added up to a great strain upon resources, and that this strategy would affect both war production and civilian morale.[29] The point here is that the indirect effects of the bombing, which would constitute one of its most important results, were being factored into the equation relatively early in the campaign. While Churchill had by now become *somewhat* less categorical in terms of enthusiastic support for the bombing, due largely to the disappointing results obtained to this point in the conflict, he was still strongly in favour of bombing the German heartland, telling Sir Archibald Sinclair that while he did not believe that bombing (alone) could decisively end the war, it was better than doing nothing, and it was "... a formidable method of injuring the enemy."[30]

CREDIT: LAC PMRC 75-346.

A de Havilland *Mosquito* bomber variant.

The next pivotal policy determinant was the release of the Singleton Report on 20 May 1942. Churchill earlier had asked Cherwell to commission an assessment of the potential value and efficacy of a concentrated area bombing campaign. The result was *The Report on the Bombing of Germany*, written by an independent assessor, Mr. Justice John Singleton. And while Singleton's report played down the view that area bombing could win the war by itself, he believed it would impede the German war effort and would also provide much-needed relief to the USSR. He asserted that Germany's war efforts could be limited and hampered by attacks upon factories engaged in war work, as well as by damage to communications grids and public utility services. Reports of the period coming in from citizens of neutral countries visiting the Third Reich tended to bolster this view. Singleton believed that significant gains could be realized by tying-down enemy resources required to defend against the bombing threat, and he opined that enemy morale was also likely to be adversely affected

DAVID L. BASHOW

by the bombing. He also saw a need for more sophisticated target identification devices, unaffected by atmospheric conditions, and additionally recommended the establishment of a specialized target identification force.[31]

Harris and his planners took great heart from these findings, although Sir Arthur disagreed with the creation of a 'stand alone' target identification force, believing this capability should be part and parcel of the individual bomb Groups. Nonetheless, Portal, as CAS, ultimately overruled Harris, and accordingly, in August, a specialized target identification and marking unit was officially established as the Pathfinder Force, #8 Group. Through trial, error, and the development and implementation of innovative techniques and equipment for target detection and marking, the Pathfinders would enhance significantly the accuracy of the Main Force bombing throughout the balance of the European war.

On an encouraging note for Bomber Command during 1942, there was a growing body of evidence that, in spite of the direct damage to German industry caused by the bombing raids, "...the most serious problem confronting the German authorities is that of re-housing the bombed-out population and providing them with clothing and other necessities of life."[32] Again, various source inputs appeared to be providing compelling proof of the validity of area bombing. Citing a well-placed clandestine source of the period, in close touch with the *Reichluftfahrtministerium* (RLM, or German Air Ministry):

> ...At the moment the fear of the RAF giant raids is far greater than any anxiety about an invasion. ...These big raids cause mass destruction. In spite of the statements in the *Wehrmacht* reports, the production of war production facilities is fairly considerable. The loss caused by the destruction of food stores and depots is extraordinarily great, as the food cannot be replaced.

The effect on the civil population of such raids is not to be underestimated.

For instance, in Köln (Cologne) there were between 3000 and 4000 dead [officially only just over 100 were reported], which of course the population of Köln knew very well. They spread the information, and this undermines confidence in the reports of the *Wehrmacht*. In Köln there were at least 200,000 persons rendered homeless, who for the most part have been evacuated, as in the city itself no new buildings or temporary premises could be erected quickly enough.

The problem of the homeless people is the most difficult. There is a shortage of houses and accommodation everywhere, in the country as well as the towns. As a result, wooden hutments have to be erected everywhere…

In the RLM there are officers of high rank and influence who seriously fear that the winter will see unrest and demonstrations, unless these mass raids are successfully dealt with. But if the SS has to be used against the civil population, a deplorable situation will arise. According to these officers the great danger is not an invasion, but the systematic destruction of German towns by the RAF.[33]

The importance of bringing forward these source documents is to make the point that the bombing offensive was evolving and developing, based upon capabilities, analysis, and direct feedback from reliable intelligence sources. Bombing policies were not being developed in a void.

An early-model Boeing B-17E *Flying Fortress.*

Friends Join the Fight

Commencing in July 1942, Britain and the Dominions would no longer find themselves alone in their bombing campaign against the Reich. With characteristic American vigour and enthusiasm, the "Mighty Eighth" Air Force of the United States Army Air Forces (USAAF) had begun a rapid build-up in southern and central Britain. Between the Eighth Air Force and the many stations occupied by Bomber Command, the little island nation was soon transformed into a vast, stationary aircraft carrier. The American contribution ultimately would be huge, and from January 1944 onwards, the Eighth Air Force would be joined by heavy bombers of the Fifteenth Air Force operating from bases in North Africa and Italy. By early August 1942, advance crews of the Eighth had been pronounced combat ready, but the British remained highly skeptical of the American daylight-only, massed formation tactics, based upon their own early war experience.[34] "They simply did not believe that the Eighth Air Force could survive daylight missions without crippling casualties. ...It would make more sense, Harris repeatedly told [Lieutenant General Ira C.] Eaker [Eighth Air Force Commander], if the Eighth would reinforce his Bomber Command by joining in the RAF's night missions."[35] On the other hand, Eaker insisted that the heavier armament his B-17s and B-24s carried could beat off the *Luftwaffe's* fighters by flying as a huge defensive entity using massed formation tactics and mutual support to defend itself to and from targets, largely without fighter escorts. And by bombing 'in the clear' in daylight, "...the US crews would be able to hit specific targets rather than being forced by darkness to dump their bomb loads helter-skelter over the blacked-out cities."[36] As the British had predicted, the blood cost of implementing these tactics would be high, particularly during the first 18 months of combat. But the loss rate would drop significantly during the last calendar year of the European war, following the introduction of the superb North American P-51 *Mustang* for long-range fighter escort to the deep German targets and back in March 1944, and once relative air superiority had been obtained over the Germans by that summer. However, the American 'precision' daylight attacks were anything *but* precise, and this will be discussed later.

B-17s in formation early in the American bombing campaign.

CREDIT: USAF Museum 070424-F-1234P-001.

DAVID L. BASHOW

Nonetheless, in spite of British concerns, the Americans were bound and determined to implement a daylight bombing strategy. At the Casablanca Conference of January 1943, a working, synergistic bond was formed that would provide the blueprint for the cooperative effort that was essentially to characterize the bomber war over Europe until the end of hostilities. After Churchill and Roosevelt had reaffirmed their overall "Germany First" plan to defeat the Reich prior to 'finishing the job' in the Pacific, a strategic compromise was struck to carry the war next to Sicily and Italy, continuing to attack the enemy on its peripheries, but postponing a cross-Channel invasion for the time being. Meanwhile, the combined forces of Britain, the Dominions, and the United States would mount a mighty Combined Bomber Offensive against targets in the Greater German Reich, the European Axis powers, and Occupied Europe. Sir Charles Portal, in particular, as Chief of the Air Staff, firmly believed that the CBO would render 25 million Germans homeless, and, more importantly, would bring war production to a complete standstill. This campaign would entail, "...the progressive destruction and dislocation of the German military, industrial and economic system, and the undermining of the morale of the German people to a point where their capacity for armed resistance is fatally weakened." Within that general concept, the primary objectives at *that* time, subject to the exigencies of weather and tactical feasibility, and in order of priority, were to be German submarine construction yards, the German aircraft industry, transportation targets, oil plants, and other targets within the enemy war industries. Every opportunity was to be taken to attack Germany by day, to destroy objectives that were not suitable for night attack (USAAF mandate), to sustain continuous pressure upon German morale, to impose heavy losses upon the German day fighter force, and to contain German fighter strength and keep it away from the Soviet and Mediterranean theatres of war.[37]

Bombing 'around the clock' became an enormous Anglo-American strategic cooperative effort which lasted – with this particular mandate unbroken – for the following sixteen months until the spring of 1944, when Bomber Command would be seconded temporarily to Supreme Headquarters Allied Expeditionary Forces (SHAEF) under General Eisenhower, flying in support of the planned D-Day landings in France. The Eighth Air Force would also fly many missions in support of the landings, although the bulk of American participation in this effort would be borne by the twin-engine medium tactical bombers of General Lewis H. Brereton's Ninth Air Force.

From this point of the war onward, the intent and the implementation of the bomber offensive are much more broadly familiar, openly documented, and better understood, although significant misconceptions still exist. Within the overall broad strategy that had been agreed upon at Casablanca, the two Anglo-American bombing armadas would place their operational emphasis upon different mandated priorities with respect to the enemy's resources at different periods of the campaign, although there was also a great amount of synergism and overlap conducted throughout. Nonetheless, until Bomber Command was seconded to SHAEF in April 1944, it tended to favour attacks upon the broader Axis industrial base, particularly the primary industries and associated infrastructure that *supplied* and *fuelled* the precision manufacturing element, such as production of coal, steel, and pig-iron, and upon transportation nodes, power sources, and mines. By contrast, the Americans preferred direct attacks upon the aircraft manufacturing and ball bearing industries, and enemy oil resources. However, readers must bear in mind that Bomber Command had already identified enemy oil as a significant target much earlier in the war, but had abandoned pursuit of this target set due to the pinpoint accuracy required to successfully attack the refineries, and the concomitant inconsistency this presented with the night area bombing strategy.

Nonetheless, the most immediate priority for the Americans was the destruction of the *Luftwaffe*. Accordingly, on 10 June 1943, nearly six months after the Casablanca Conference, the resulting Joint Chiefs directive was modified to acknowledge the growing strength of the German air defences, and to target specifically the German day fighter arm in a range of bombing options. "The German fighter force was given the status of 'intermediate target,' and its destruction was made the primary goal. The campaign was given the unambiguous codename *Pointblank*."[38] It tasked both the American forces and Bomber Command with:

- The destruction of German airframe, engine and component factories and the ball bearing industry on which the strength of the German fighter force depend;

- The general disorganization of those industrial areas associated with the above industries;

- The destruction of those aircraft repair depots and storage tanks within range, and on which the enemy fighter force is largely dependent; and

- The destruction of enemy fighters in the air and on the ground.[39]

While Bomber Command continued to feel the stinging power of the German fighter arm, Harris tended, as was his wont, to view the German aircraft industry as 'panacea' targets, and while he would not ignore them, he generally applied his priorities elsewhere, such as through the aforementioned 'general disorganization' clause, leaving the bulk of the specific *Pointblank* targets to the Americans. That said, in his book, *Fire and Fury*, and in related articles, Randall Hansen has referred to the defeat of the *Luftwaffe* as being almost entirely an American accomplishment, with only token help from Bomber Command. This is both naïve and uninformed. The destruction of the *Luftwaffe* was truly a synergistic effort conducted, not merely by the strategic air forces of Britain and America, but also by the Allied Tactical Air Forces (ATAFs), and, especially, by their respective fighter commands.

That said, Bomber Command certainly pulled its weight with direct attacks upon German aircraft (and component) production facilities and storage and communication facilities, and this reality is amply reinforced by even a cursory review of Bomber Command's wartime operational diaries. Furthermore, the continuous luring into combat and the concomitant destruction of enemy fighter forces necessitated by enemy fighter defensive actions against the bombing raids, day and night, dealt telling blows to the *Luftwaffe's* day and night fighter arms.

Bombing to Win

Thus commenced in earnest the great, cooperative aerial onslaught against Adolf Hitler's *Festung Europa* (Fortress Europe), and before it was over, due in no small measure to the resounding air superiority that would be attained eventually during the campaign, the Third Reich would become a ruined fortress without a roof. It would result in over *two million tons* of ordnance being dropped upon European Axis targets. However, it would also demand a very high toll in aircrew blood, including over 81,000 total wartime aircrew fatalities from just Bomber Command and the Eighth Air Force.[40]

CREDIT: LAC PMR 93-293.

Part of the human cost of the bomber offensive.

Earlier, Sir Arthur Harris had waged what he believed to be a very successful campaign against Hamburg in June 1943,[41] and just prior to that, a concentrated series of attacks against the industrialized Ruhr, the so-called Second Battle of the Ruhr. He continued to be focused relentlessly in his belief that the German people would crack under the strain of the city attacks, negating the need for a bloody and costly invasion. This mindset was fuelled largely by the results obtained from those bombings, particularly that of Hamburg, which had produced extensive damage, generated an artificial firestorm, and produced an estimated 45,000 fatal casualties. And perhaps due to undue weight being given to a flow of intelligence reports citing civil unrest, which fostered a belief that this would erupt into a popular general uprising, such as had occurred in Italy during the summer of 1943, Harris opined, "We can wreck Berlin from end to end if the USAAF will come in on it. It will cost us between 400-500 aircraft. It will cost Germany the war."[42] This was naïve on a number of counts, particularly with respect to expectations of a popular uprising and the overthrow of a government that ruled ruthlessly by the spur of terror in a total police state, using cruelty to dominate, to subjugate, and to enforce its policies, and to quell any and all dissent and opposition. Furthermore, the USAAF would not attack Berlin in earnest until the spring of 1944 and beyond, and although much significant damage had been done to the Nazi epicentre during Bomber Command's siege, the capital had held firm. Harris's gallant crews, while they had persevered steadfastly, had nonetheless been highly demoralized by their long-standing, relentless trail of combat losses. As it materialized, the upcoming secondment to SHAEF, with much fewer deep penetration targets assigned, a progressive rollback and substantial deterioration of enemy air defences, and a significant further build-up of personnel and materiel resources during the secondment period from April to September 1944, would, beyond doubt, become the ultimate salvation of aircrew morale within Bomber Command, and it would also mark a turnabout in its effectiveness.

Anglo-American Differences of Opinion over the Importance of Enemy Oil

A significant point of divergence between Bomber Command and the USSTAF was the importance initially allocated to oil as a priority target. Furthermore, this divergence eventually would lead to a confrontation between Sir Charles Portal, as Chief of the Air Staff, and Sir Arthur Harris in his role as Bomber Command's helmsman. By late-September 1944, once the land campaign had stagnated in northwest Europe and the strategic bomber forces had been returned to the fold of their respective air staffs, Harris sensed that an unrestricted return to his general area bombing campaign of the German industrial heartland was in the wind. However, an Air Staff Directive of 25 September 1944 stated Bomber Command's new targeting priorities as follows:

First Priority

- Petroleum industry, with special emphasis upon petrol (gasoline) including storage.

Second Priority

- The German rail and waterborne transportation systems.

- Tank production plants and depots, ordnance depots.

- Motorized Transport (MT) production plants and depots.[43]

For the immediate future, although earlier counter-air action no longer had any particular priority, *relative* air superiority having now been attained, the generalized city offensive was only to be undertaken when conditions were unfavourable to executing the new priorities. These new priorities certainly suited General Spaatz, since oil, which had been a priority target for the Americans since the summer of 1943, had been placed squarely in the highest position by the British Air Staff, which, by the autumn of 1944, had warmed to the American point of view. Furthermore, Air Chief Marshal Sir Arthur Tedder, Eisenhower's deputy at SHAEF, believed that the plan should be broadened by synergistic linkage to attacks upon all the enemy's means of conveyance, "…to attack all communications, railways, rivers and canals as well, thus strangling industry, government control, life itself. Concentrated on such an area as the Ruhr, and linked to a powerful ground offensive, Tedder was convinced this would be decisive."[44] Portal and his staff were in accord with this thinking, and it was once again Harris who appeared to be out of synchronization. To Harris, oil remained the hated 'panacea' he had perceived it to be from the outset, especially given the Soviet capture of Ploesti and the other Rumanian oil fields in August 1944, the concomitant denial of Rumanian oil to the Axis powers, and the fact that Bomber Command had *already* expended, as we have seen, considerable time and effort with respect to enemy oil. According to Harris's biographer, Air Commodore Henry Probert:

> He [Harris] was still deeply suspicious of the prognostications of the Ministry of Economic Warfare; synthetic oil production was spread over many plants, often small, in different parts of Germany, and up-to-date intelligence about them was hard to obtain; the Germans under Speer were adept at dispersal and repair; and effective attacks required a degree of accuracy which he was far from convinced his aircraft could achieve, especially against more distant targets.[45]

CREDIT: USAF Museum 080721-F-1234P-004.

Incendiaries rain down upon a German industrial city.

To regress slightly, during the run-up to Operation *Overlord* in June, and in the weeks immediately following the landings, an overall loss rate of 11 percent of the 832 Bomber Command aircraft dispatched against ten synthetic oil plants on a trial basis to the Ruhr industrialized area on three separate operations, including a devastating 27.8 percent loss rate on a 20/21 June operation, had done nothing to convince Harris that these were either sensible or appropriate targets. However, after these exploratory raids, a second round of attacks launched in July was less costly, and by August, the Air Ministry was convinced that oil was a legitimate Number One priority. Nonetheless, personal entreaties by Harris to Churchill led to what Harris believed was qualified approval from the PM for a resumption of the area bombing of the cities,[46] and consequently, Bomber Command devoted only six percent of its bomb tonnage against oil targets in October 1944. That said, the USAAF did little better, contributing only 10 percent of its monthly effort in kind. However, it was at precisely this time that intelligence reports indicated – and they were later proven to be correct – that Germany's oil situation was at its most desperate juncture. While official historians from the United States, Britain, and Australia have all contended that more ought to have been done against enemy oil during this period, given the 'hitting power' of the Anglo-American forces by this time and the significant weakening of the enemy air defences, the weather during the autumn months was very poor. In fact, the historians also concur that, "...there were few occasions when oil targets could be visually bombed, and not many tactical opportunities were in fact missed."[47] Further, even the USAAF official history states that by the end of November 1944, the weight of effort by Bomber Command against the oil targets was actually exceeding that of the Americans, and they were proving to be both successful and effective. It goes on to say that the results obtained against the oil industry during the last months of 1944 were spectacular, and were "... more effective in terms of destruction than most Allied experts had dared to hope."[48] However, many sharp exchanges would take place between Portal and Harris in late 1944 and continue into early 1945 over the latter's perceived lack of compliance with the Combined Chiefs and Air Staff Directives with respect to oil.[49] Nonetheless, by year's end, Bomber Command would place considerably more weight of effort behind the Oil Plan.[50] Furthermore, while Harris continued undeterred with area bombing until the end of hostilities, in spite of perceived differences between Portal and Harris, area bombing would enjoy Portal's support until the very end of the war. Henry Probert sums up the issue with the following comments:

> As Harris himself later recognized, oil did prove more critical
> than he had judged at the time. Influenced by the views of

> Albert Speer, Hitler's Armament Minister, he wrote in 1947
> that in the final weeks of the war all the German armed forces
> had been immobilized for lack of fuel, rendering the triumph
> of the oil offensive complete and indisputable. It was the one
> 'panacea' that actually paid off.[51]

Nonetheless, there is no doubting the ultimate success of the Oil Plan, and it remains an unanswerable question as to just how much the European war could have been shortened had Harris embraced the plan with more enthusiasm at the outset. That said, as has been demonstrated throughout this text, and in spite of the aforementioned differences of opinion, the counter-oil campaign was a highly success-ful cooperative effort, and Professor Hansen's failure to acknowledge Bomber Command's prosecution of this target *throughout the war* is misplaced.

The War against Enemy Transportation

An earlier joint effort known as the Transportation Plan also proved to be a very effective precursor to the Normandy landings. Designed to disrupt rail communications by attacking some 74 key rail centres in France and Belgium as an obvious Operation *Overlord* priority, on 15 April 1944, Bomber Command was allocated 37 of the rail targets, the other half being assigned to the Americans. By the eve of D-Day, some 60 separate attacks had put at least two-thirds of the assigned Bomber Command targets out of action for a minimum of a month. Further, the cost in civilian collateral casualties had been kept well below the 10,000 total that both Churchill and Portal fervently hoped would not be exceeded.[52] So successful was the plan's implementation that "...after the Allied landings had taken place, scarcely any enemy fortifications could be brought into action without lengthy detours or delays, a factor which proved critical during the vital consolidation of the invasion beachheads."[53] And continued, unrelenting pressure by the strategic bombing forces upon Axis road, rail, and waterways from this point onwards until the end of hostilities would yield very tangible results against an enemy transportation network that was already stretched to the limit, due to dynamic and changing operational requirements, and to the tremendous additional burden of forced industrial decentralization, which had been brought about by the bombings.

With respect to the *overall* transportation campaign, Professor Hansen in his writings has grossly understated this contribution to victory by Bomber Command, while concurrently overstating the American contribution. The Command's *deliberate* bombing of industrial city centres from early in the war generated a high, prolonged, and sustained degree of damage to core road and rail assets; a much more concentrated degree of damage than that waged by the sporadic attacks of the Americans until they specifically targeted enemy city centres on a broader scale somewhat later in the war. Downstream from the pre-*Overlord* attacks, Bomber Command devoted extensive resources against enemy transportation networks and facilities. Perhaps none was more effective than the attacks upon the German waterway systems, particularly those on the Rhine River and the Dortmund Ems Canal. During the last four months of the war, Bomber Command devoted 15.4 percent of its total efforts (28,102 tons of bombs) against enemy transportation assets. And between October 1944 and March 1945, the attacks on both rail and water transportation networks were so effective that the Germans could scarcely manage 12 percent of throughput of critical resources to the industrialized Ruhr, and this included the near-total curtailment of coal.[54] Also due to strategic bombing, the virtual collapse of the transportation networks by 1945 meant that Germany's still-enormous field armies could no longer be reliably supplied or armed.

CREDIT: LAC PL30780.

A *Halifax* III attacking a V-1 rocket launch site in France.

Pounding the Reich

It was during the last calendar year of the war that Bomber Command reached its most productive, albeit destructive apex. Back on 3 November 1942, as a precursor to the Casablanca Conference, Portal, with a major input from Harris, had presented the British Chiefs of Staff with a blueprint for a joint Anglo-American bombing offensive, which assumed a combined bomber fleet of 4000-6000 aircraft available at all times, upon which to base their bombing strategy.[55] And the last calendar year of the European war was decisive for the strategic bombing campaign, with over two-thirds of the total wartime bomb tonnage being dropped on the Greater German Reich from July 1944 onwards.[56] Also, along with vastly declining German defensive capabilities, due in no small measure to the overrunning of German early warning sites in the land battle for the Continent, for Bomber Command, the monthly average number of sorties increased from 5400 in 1943 to 14,000 in 1944, and the average payload-per-sortie nearly

DAVID L. BASHOW

doubled.[57] And from the summer of 1944 onwards, once relative air superiority had been attained over Northwest Europe, Bomber Command would complement its nocturnal sorties with more and more daylight operations.

At this point, the frequently misunderstood concepts of American *precision daylight* bombing and British *night area* bombing need to be addressed and placed within a proper context, due in no small measure to the fundamentally erroneous conclusions Professor Hansen has reached with respect to American capabilities and execution.

At the end of September 1944, Harris remained unconvinced that attacks upon the 'panacea' targets of oil, transportation, and the tank industry, for example, could damage the enemy's war making capability as much as broader, renewed attacks upon the industrial cities. Accordingly, the so-called Third Battle of the Ruhr deserves special mention for its brief intensity and focus, since these raids were planned as joint Bomber Command/USSTAF area attacks, designed to scuttle enemy war efforts in a region directly facing the Allied land armies. Perhaps the most famous of these raids was a coordinated area attack upon the industrial cities of Duisburg and Cologne on 14/15 October, commencing with a daylight raid on Duisburg by the RAF at dawn, followed by a force of 1251 bombers from the Eighth Air Force against Cologne, and then a night raid by 941 aircraft from Bomber Command against Duisburg. By the time the bombers had finished, extensive damage from area bombing had been meted out to Cologne, and Duisburg had essentially been reduced to rubble, producing substantial damage to the Thyssen and Duisburg-Hamborn mines and coke ovens. And 10,500 tons of bombs had been dropped on Duisburg alone, "… record totals that would never be exceeded in the war."[58]

On the night of 23/24 October 1944, and again the following day, it was Essen's turn to be pounded. The night raid was mounted by 1055 aircraft, including 561 *Lancasters*, 463 *Halifaxes*, and 31 *Mosquitos*.

Unlike the thousand-bomber raids of 1942, this time no crews from training units had to be included in order to put so many machines in the air. Moreover, all those that participated were four-engined "heavies," so that a greater weight of bombs was delivered. Bombing through cloud, the attackers caused "extensive damage" to a complex of Krupp factories but lost only twelve crews... Thirty-six hours later a daylight raid brought 771 raiders back to the same target. Essen, like many other German cities, was now little more than a heap of rubble.[59]

While parts of Essen's steel industry had already been moved to dispersed factories, "...the Krupps steelworks were particularly hard hit by the two raids, and there were references in the firm's archives to the 'almost complete breakdown of the electrical supply network' and to 'a complete paralysis.' The Borbeck pig-iron plant ceased work completely and there is no record of any further production from this important section of Krupps."[60]

Canadian airmen send Christmas greetings to the Third Reich.

The late-war *Thunderclap* and *Clarion* plans also merit mention, since these were area attacks conducted by *both* the USSTAF and Bomber Command. The genesis of the *Clarion* plan, eventually an all-out attack on German transportation – railway yards and stations – originated with the original *Thunderclap* plan, an early-August 1944 proposal by the Air Ministry for a massive joint strike on Berlin, "…[in] the hope that it would make Hitler's people see sense; this was shortly after the July bomb attempt on Hitler's life had revealed that support for the Führer was not as solid as people supposed."[61] Essentially, it called for a massive, daylight strike on the German capital by the USAAF, followed up by the RAF with a night raid of equal proportions. Failing the acceptability of this, it called for widespread attacks upon cities across Germany in an attempt to convince the German people that further resistance was futile. The USAAF senior commanders and authorities in Washington rejected *Thunderclap* in its original form on 16 August 1944, but Spaatz was willing to assist *Thunderclap* through precision attacks on Berlin, and by 8 September, he was telling the commander of the Eighth Air Force, General Doolittle, that American forces would no longer plan to hit definite military objectives, but would be ready to drop bombs indiscriminately on Berlin.[62] In fact, by autumn, General Arnold had directed the USSTAF – Spaatz – to prepare plans for an all-out attack upon Germany, "…widespread roving attacks so that all Germans could see the ease with which Allied airpower roamed at will through the airspace of the Reich."[63] Although the German Ardennes offensive delayed this initiative, by January 1945, Spaatz was ready, and "…the all-out attack on transportation [*Clarion*] had been extended to include a smashing blow against Berlin."[64]

On 3 February 1945, just such a "smashing blow" occurred. Bombing in clear air over the capital, 937 Eighth Air Force B-17s attacked the Berlin railway system in the belief that the German Sixth Panzer Army was moving through Berlin on its way to the Eastern Front.[65] In the words of the 303rd Bomb Group's official combat mission report, "About three-fourths of the lead squadron[s] bombs hit in the fully built-up central city area with the balance hitting in the compact residential area."[66] While the initial number of civilian casualties was grossly exaggerated at 25,000 fatalities and fed to the world through lurid German accounts to the Swedish press, the actual number of fatalities is now believed to have been not more than one-eighth of that number, between 2500 and 3000, with 120,000 persons "dehoused."[67] Another USAAF area attack on Berlin on 26 February, this time conducted 'blind' through a thick undercast, caused further extensive damage, loss of life, and the 'dehousing' of an additional 80,000 inhabitants. In the words of Charles P. Johnson of the 303rd Bomb Group:

> 26 February 1945 began with an early wake-up call and the briefing that day was for Berlin – the 'Big B' – which the briefing officer assured us was not the formidable target it had been earlier in the war. The real shock came when he told us we were to bomb from the east. We flew east, past Berlin, and then turned 180° in order to bomb into the wind, which, with the strong headwinds, took us over the city at around 35 knots groundspeed, which seemed like an eternity in range of the anti-aircraft guns, but because of the cloud cover and the fact that we bombed from 25,000 feet, we encountered only ineffective flak. The bomb drop was by means of radar and we were unable to observe the result, but since the target was the marshalling yards within the city, we assumed that we accomplished some damage to the enemy.[68]

In point of fact, from late-1944 onwards, both the British and the Americans were conducting significant amounts of area bombing, or 'blind bombing,' as it was referred to in USAAF circles. From the official USAAF history:

> Approximately 80 percent of all Eighth Air Force and 70 percent of all Fifteenth Air Force missions during the last

quarter of 1944 were characterized by some employment of blind-bombing radar devices. Without these aids important targets would have enjoyed weeks or months of respite and on several occasions major task forces failed even with radar to reach their objectives because of adverse weather... In mid-November 1944, operations analysts of the Eighth estimated that nearly half the blind missions were near failures, or worse.[69]

Richard Overy takes this point even farther.

The US air forces soon abandoned any pretence that they could bomb with precision, and two-thirds of their bombs were dropped blind through cloud and smog. A staggering 87 percent of all bombs missed their target.[70]

CREDIT: USAF Museum 060517-F-12345-051

B-17s formating among marker flares.

The American historian Tami Davis Biddle, a professor at the US Army War College and a subject matter expert, also elaborates:

Even though the Americans strongly *preferred* to strike specific industrial sites (and flew to those whenever weather permitted), the bulk of their raids through cloud were, in essence, area raids. In order to distinguish their efforts from those of the British, however, the Americans continued to use language that depicted them as "precision" bombing of specific military targets.[71]

And while the number and strength of American area attacks certainly increased during the last calendar year of the war, area attacks by the Americans were, in fact, common practice even earlier in the bombing campaign, and these were conducted both in clear air and through cloud, guided by dedicated Pathfinder aircraft. Joel Punches flew combat operations as a navigator in B-17Fs with the 385th Bomb Wing of the Eighth Air Force out of Great Ashfield, England, between 5 September 1943 and 21 February 1944. Readers should note that this period was characterized by particularly heavy loss rates to the American forces as they persevered in their daylight operations. The diary entries of Punches make particularly interesting reading with respect to the lack of specific military objectives associated with the targets on many of the missions, bearing in mind that these words were penned at the very time the missions occurred, and not years after the fact.

- 2 October 1943 ~ Emden, Germany. Transportation center in northern Germany. Bombed through clouds using Pathfinder leader.

- 10 October 1943 ~ Munster, Germany. Entirely wiped out Munster. Clear and visibility good. Group ahead dropped demolition (high explosive) bombs on the business district and we followed with incendiary bombs. Twenty minutes after we left it was a mass of flames and smoke… Hitler must really be tearing his hair now. [We] seem to like to bomb on Sunday. Get them all together in the churches. Our bombs hit in a beautiful pattern – all concentrated and really worth the trouble, for a change…

- 14 October 1943 ~ Schweinfurt, Germany. Ball bearing works. How we ever got back from this one I still don't understand! … Carried incendiaries. Clear over target and when we left it was a huge mass of flames. The whole town was burning…

- 18 October 1943 ~ Duren, Germany. A town of 50,000 people. Not much military importance. Just wanted to wipe out the town. Morale raid, I guess…

- 19 November 1943 ~ Gelsenkirchen, Germany. In the Ruhr valley. Rail junction and business district of town. Flew for an hour over Germany and Pathfinder ship couldn't find the target, so we dumped our bombs on a small town and came home. The town dropped on turned out to be a town in Holland. Not so good!

- 24 November 1943 ~ Berlin, Germany. Mean Point of Impact (MPI) was the Air Ministry building in the center of Berlin, but the mission was scrubbed (weather)

- 30 November 1943 ~ Solingen, Germany. Town of 150,000. MPI was business district.

- 12 December 1943 ~ Kiel, Germany. Germany's North Sea Fleet's harbor. City of 250,000. Germany was closed over so the Pathfinder was used. Dropped our bombs on the Pathfinder over Kiel.

- 15 December 1943 ~ Bremen, Germany. Rail center and manufacturing center. Pathfinder mission with mixed load of incendiary and demolition bombs.

- 19 December 1943 ~ Bremen, Germany. Carried 36 incendiary bombs. MPI was the business district. Every division hit Bremen square in the city. Our group bombardier synchronized on a large church. When we left, the city was burning amid a cloud of smoke.

- 18 January 1944 ~ Frankfurt, Germany. MPI business district of town. City of 500,000 people. Pathfinder mission. Dropped bombs using the Pathfinder and pretty sure we hit the city...

- 19 January 1944 ~ Braunschweig, Germany. City of 500,000 population. Carried twelve 500 pound demolition bombs. Pathfinder mission. During the bomb run, the high squadron was directly over us and we had to move around to prevent their dropping on us. Scared us plenty...

- 24 January 1944 ~ Wilhelmshaven, Germany. Target was center of town.

- 4 February 1944 ~ Frankfurt, Germany. We carried ten 500 pound demolition bombs. MPI was the old business district of town.[72]

In their defence, weather conditions over the European continent were forcing the blind bombing option upon both camps. It is ironic, however, that while the USAAF had commenced making area attacks in earnest from 1944 onwards, Bomber Command was now making precision attacks, both night and day, upon specific military and industrial targets. Technological advances abounded. *G-H* represented a quantum leap in the development of navigation systems, since it combined levels of accuracy comparable to *Oboe* with the universal applicability of *Gee*. It had been introduced to service by 3 Group in 1943, and it was used to effect eventually by other formations. Around the same time, the K-band *H2S* Mark VI radar was also fielded, and this alleviated some system limitations over poorly defined or obscured targets.[73]

Bomber Command coupled these new devices with revised tactics. Navigation was now so accurate that decoy fires and spoof raids could be used within a few miles of the actual route. The navigators and bomb-aimers were now sufficiently skilled to use an offset bombing point chosen for its visibility, and to aim their bombs at a given range and bearing from that point.[74]

Night attack on Nuremburg, 27/28 August 1943.

The Final Round

By 1945, marking techniques in Bomber Command had reached new levels of maturity and sophistication, including the increasing use of offset tactics. Now, although the Main Force journeymen aimed for a single marking reference on a given target, different approach angles, combined with timed overshoots, provided a number of actual release points on every successful attack. The offset procedure reduced the predictability, and thus the vulnerability of the attacking bombers. Also, multiple streams consisting of simultaneous large-scale efforts on different targets were common by 1945, further confusing the defences and further reducing predictability. By this stage of the war, given the predominating weather over the continent, Bomber Command had acquired so much expertise in blind bombing and the innovative use of radar and other electronic aids that its crews were generally as comfortable bombing in obscured conditions at night, with comparable results, as they were when bombing 'in the clear' by daylight. For their part, after the Schweinfurt-Regensburg raids, the Americans accepted that weather, navigation, and target finding were significant problems affecting operations:

> Here again, [the Americans] had the benefit of RAF experience and cooperation. The two air forces had always worked closely together, and this liaison now paid off. It was accepted that, since European weather was frequently poor, 'blind bombing' was inevitable, even in daylight, and the *Gee*-box and *H2S* – known to the Eighth as *H2X* or 'Mickey' – were introduced into US aircraft.[75]

By early 1944, the Eighth Air Force had come to rely extensively upon 'blind' attacking targets by *Oboe* and by *H2X*. In fact, "...on only one occasion in six weeks [during January and early February 1944] were the skies clear enough for visual bombing."[76] And that reliance upon electronic aids would only increase during the rest of the bombing campaign. By early 1945, in a further broad distillation of precision bombardment, and a tacit acknowledgement that area attacks had become accepted American strategy, a new crew member known as the 'togglier' frequently replaced the much more extensively trained (and usually commissioned) bombardier within American bomber crews.

> [On the Berlin mission 18 March 1945] I was flying as a togglier (enlisted bombardier who threw the switch to release bombs). When the lead bombardier's Norden bombsight released his bombs, two smoke bomb[s] were released from below the chin turret. When the rest of the squadron bombardiers or toggliers saw the smoke bombs released we then hit the Salvo switch and released our bombs also. Of course, milliseconds later we would have seen the actual explosive bombs falling from the bomb-bay, but in an attempt to group the bombs on target we needed to release them almost at the same time the lead bombardier released his bombs.

> ~ Hal Province
> 391st Bomb Squadron,
> 34th Bomb Group[77]

The Issue of Enemy Morale

Meanwhile, *Thunderclap* had certainly evolved from just being the massive, joint attack upon Berlin that had been initially envisaged.

> By 1945, the Air Staff considered that *Thunderclap* might well appear to the Germans as an excellent example of close coordination with the Russians, thereby greatly increasing the morale effect. In January 1945, the Joint Intelligence Committee (JIC) played down the possibility of German resistance crumbling, but highlighted the scope for confusion in the movement of reinforcements and refugees

if, by implication, critical towns in the infrastructure were attacked… The JIC report coincided with preparations for the Allied discussions in Malta that were the precursor to the Yalta conference with the Soviets. In the meantime, Churchill had asked the Secretary of State for Air, Sir Archibald Sinclair, what plans he had for "…basting the Germans in their retreat from Breslau."[78]

CREDIT: LAC PL33337.

The strain of sustained operations shows on this young pilot's face.

DAVID L. BASHOW

Sir Charles Portal then advised Sinclair that *Thunderclap*, as it originally had been conceived, undoubtedly would be both costly and indecisive, and instead recommended the continued absolute priority of oil targets, the submarine yards, and the jet aircraft factories. However, Portal also endorsed the sentiments of the January JIC Report and recommended specific attacks on Berlin, Chemnitz, Dresden, Leipzig, "…or any other cities where a severe blitz will not only cause confusion in the evacuation from the East, but will also hamper the movement of troops from the West."[79] Sinclair then cautiously responded to the Prime Minister, "You asked me last night whether we had any plans for harrying the German retreat from Breslau." He said that oil should remain the paramount priority, but that secondary option attacks could be considered against Eastern German cities when poor weather would not permit attacks against oil infrastructure. He reiterated specifically the cities mentioned by Portal, stating that not only were they the main administrative centres controlling military and civilian movements in the region, but they were also the main communications centres through which the bulk of all traffic flowed. Sinclair then closed with, "To achieve results of real value, a series of heavy attacks would probably be required, and weather conditions at this time of year would certainly prevent these being delivered in quick succession. The possibility of these attacks being delivered on the scale necessary to have a critical effect on the situation in Eastern Germany is now under examination."[80] Churchill's particularly testy response to Sinclair is worth quoting in full:

Serial No M.115/5

SECRETARY OF STATE FOR AIR

I did not ask you last night about plans for harrying the German retreat from Breslau. On the contrary, I asked whether Berlin, and no doubt other large cities in East Germany, should not now be considered especially attractive targets. I am glad that this is "under examination." Pray report to me tomorrow what is going to be done.

W.S.C.
26/1/45[81]

The unequivocal tone of this correspondence generated the following immediate response from Sinclair to his Prime Minister:

TOP SECRET

PRIME MINISTER

Your Minute M.115/5. The Air Staff have now arranged that, subject to the overriding claims of attacks on enemy oil production and other approved target systems within the current directive, available effort should be directed against Berlin, Dresden, Chemnitz and Leipzig or against other cities where severe bombing would not only destroy communications vital to the evacuation from the East but would also hamper the movement of troops from the West.

The use of the night bomber force offers the best prospects of destroying these industrial cities without detracting from our offensive on oil targets, which is now in a critical phase. The Air Officer Commanding-in-Chief, Bomber Command, has undertaken to attempt this task as soon as the present moon has waned and favourable weather conditions allow. This is unlikely to be before about 4th February.

A.S.
27th January 1945[82]

CREDIT: LAC PL22031.

The loneliest job. A *Halifax* rear gunner.

Simultaneously, Portal's Deputy Chief of the Air Staff, Sir Norman Bottomley, formally instructed Harris to carry out the specified attacks. A series of meetings between Portal, Tedder, Bottomley, and General Spaatz reconfirmed oil as the Number One bombing priority for strategic bombing forces in Britain. This would, in turn, be followed by attacks on Berlin, Dresden, and Leipzig, which included the destruction of communications nodes servicing the respective fronts. Finally, there were the jet aircraft production plants. The Vice-Chiefs in London gave their blessings to these priorities and also added a demand for a more sustained effort against enemy tank production facilities. Thus, that portion of the bomber offensive known as *Thunderclap* was officially born within those other priorities, and, in concert with parallel daylight operations by the USAAF known as *Clarion*, it would consist of a series of punishing raids against the remaining industrialized German centres, designed primarily to disrupt enemy communications and transportation capabilities, but also to deal major blows to enemy morale.[83]

> The plot now moves to Yalta where the debate over who said what to whom becomes complex. Cold War Soviet propaganda has emphasized that the Russian delegation in the Crimea had no responsibility for the bombing of Dresden. The Allies were unequivocal in their inclusion of Dresden in the target list, in particular with its importance on the Berlin-Leipzig-Dresden railway. The Russian Deputy Chief of Staff, General Antonov, submitted a formal memorandum to the Allies requesting, inter alia, that air attacks against communications should be carried out, "…in particular to paralyze the centres: Berlin and Leipzig." The use of the wording "in particular" makes it, at best, disingenuous for the Russians subsequently to suggest that they had not requested action at Dresden.[84]

Tami Davis Biddle elaborates:

> During the Yalta discussions, the Russians specifically requested raids against Berlin and Leipzig to help block German movement of troops to the east. In general, though, they were cautious, arguing for a bombing line that would run from Berlin to Dresden, and Vienna to Zagreb. Though these cities could be included in Anglo-American strike plans, the Russians wanted everything east of the line kept off limits. On this point, see also Henry Probert, *Bomber Harris: His Life and Times* (London: Greenhill Books, 2001), p. 319, who argues that while the formal record cites only Berlin and Leipzig as the specific requests, Hugh Lunghi, the Russian language interpreter for the British Chiefs of Staff, was certain that the Russians had also requested the bombing of Dresden. Probert interviewed Lunghi on this point in 2000, and cites as well Lunghi's letter to the British journal, *The*

Spectator, of 6 August 1994, arguing that Stalin himself had requested bombing of the city. Lunghi wrote: "I was present at the meeting of the British, United States and Soviet Chiefs of Staff on 5 February [1945] in the Yusupov Palace, Stalin's headquarters... when the Soviet Chiefs requested the Allies to deliver massive attacks on German communications in the Berlin-Leipzig-Dresden area and specifically to bomb those cities urgently" Finally, see Taylor, *Dresden*, pp. 190-192.[85]

Operations by both Bomber Command and the USAAF on 13/14 February resulted in massive destruction and loss of life, although the casualties were grossly exaggerated from the outset. Conditions combined to produce a true firestorm, one of just three that occurred in the European theatre, the others being at Hamburg in July 1943, and then at Kassel in October 1943.

Dresden... The city and its very name has become a 'poster child' for the opponents of the area bombing campaign, but there is a lot of 'mythology' that has been generated over these late-war raids. While it is true that the bombing destroyed much property and thousands of German lives, the number of fatalities was greatly exaggerated from the outset (by a factor of up to 1000 percent) in an extremely effective propaganda campaign waged by the German Propaganda Ministry through the neutral countries and the United States.[86]

And contrary to popular belief, Dresden in 1945 was far more than just a beautiful baroque centre of cultural significance. It was also an armed camp, and, most importantly, a vital communications and transportation hub, and a control node for the resupply and sustainment of Eastern Front operations. It also played host to scores of embedded factories producing goods vital to the German war effort, including the massive Zeiss-Ikon complex. And it had been a long time since Zeiss-Ikon had produced anything as innocent as a holiday snapshot camera.[87]

Worthy of note, on 2 October 2008, in the German periodical *Der Spiegel*, noted British historian Frederick Taylor observed:

> Now, more than 60 years later, it seems we must lower our estimates [of casualties at Dresden – DB]. After four year's work, an impressive commission of German historians [including the renowned Dr. Horst Boog – DB] this week filed its report on this issue, and it seems that even the lowest figure so far accepted may be an overestimate. Drawing on archival sources, many never previously consulted, on burial grounds and scientific findings – including street-by-street archaeological investigations – plus hundreds of eyewitness reports, the 'Dresden Commission of Historians for the Ascertainment of the Number of Victims of the Air Raids on the city of Dresden on 13/14 February 1945' has provisionally estimated the likely death toll at around 18,000 and definitely no more than 25,000.[88]

Air Chief Marshal Harris and his planners get ready for a raid.

CREDIT: IWM HU44269.

A Certain Duplicity

By the spring of 1945, the eddies of public disquiet generated by the bombing of Dresden with respect to Anglo-American bombing policy were swirling. Just six weeks after the February raids, Winston Churchill, perhaps with an eye cast towards his legacy, penned a Minute to Lord Ismay, his military advisor to the Chiefs of Staff Committee, and to the Chief of the Air Staff in particular, which Bomber Command's official historians would later consider "…perhaps the least felicitous," well-expressed, or appropriate of all Churchill's wartime correspondence.[89] The Minute appeared to endorse all the latest public criticism of Allied bombing policy, and it also seemed to shift the blame from the prime minister's shoulders to those of the air commanders responsible for implementing the policy. The implication was that Churchill had been misled and that his air leaders were conducting terror bombing on their own initiative, without his knowledge, but both these conditions were patently false, as has been thoroughly documented herein.[90]

Serial No D. 83/5

TOP SECRET

GENERAL ISMAY FOR C.O.S. COMMITTEE
C.A.S.

It seems to me that the moment has come when the question of bombing of German cities simply for the sake of increasing the terror, though under other pretexts, should be reviewed. Otherwise, we shall come into control of an utterly ruined land. We shall not, for instance, be able to get housing materials out of Germany for our own needs because some temporary provision would have to be made for Germans themselves. The destruction of Dresden remains a serious query against the conduct of the Allied bombing. I am of the opinion that military objectives must henceforward be more strictly studied in our own interests rather than that of the enemy.

The Foreign Secretary has spoken to me on this subject, and I feel the need for more precise concentration upon military objectives, such as Oil and communications behind the immediate battle zone, rather than on mere acts of terror and wanton destruction, however impressive.

W.S.C.

28.3.45 [91]

A late-war attack on the fortress island of Wangerooge, 25 April 1945.

Sir Charles Portal immediately instructed his deputy, Sir Norman Bottomley, to solicit Sir Arthur Harris's comments. The Bomber Command helmsman's reply was prompt, as well as characteristically blunt and predictable. He pointed out:

...that the suggestion that the bomber offensive had been conducted "for the sake of increasing terror, though under other pretexts" was an insult both to the Air Ministry policy and to the crews that had carried it out. Harris went on to highlight the misperceptions over Dresden that would be obvious to any psychiatrist – "...it is connected to German bands and Dresden shepherdesses." Rather, "Dresden was a mass of munitions works, an intact government centre and a key transportation point to the East. It is now none of these things."[92]

Harris also observed that the bombing of the industrialized cities had fatally impaired the overall German war effort and was permitting the land forces to advance into Germany with fewer casualties than expected. He argued that it would be a mistake to totally cease these attacks at the time unless it could be said with absolute certainty that eliminating city bombing would shorten the war and save the lives of Allied soldiers. Then, he made a somewhat insensitive remark, borrowing and building upon the words of Prussia's "Iron Chancellor," Prince Otto von Bismarck: "I do not personally regard the whole of the remaining cities of Germany as worth the bones of one British grenadier."[93] Harris, in his no-nonsense response, when asked his opinions, probably never thought this correspondence, which had been marked at the time both "Personal" and "Top Secret," would one day be made available for public scrutiny and subject to the endless parsing of armchair strategists and moralists. Furthermore, his primary consideration, after getting the job done to the best of Bomber Command's abilities, was to minimize the risks incurred to his aircrews, who had endured steadfastly so much hardship during the war.[94]

Churchill also appears to have exercised a conveniently selective memory when he penned the offending Minute, choosing to ignore the various telephone conversations, memos, and directives to Sir

Archibald Sinclair in January, which had urged bombing attacks upon the eastern cities.

Churchill was well aware that the RAF was going to attack Dresden and the other eastern cities; the decision to do so had originated in Cabinet and had his full support. To deny it now did him no credit and was clearly an attempt to distance himself and his government from the political fallout among the neutral countries and in the USA. The comment, "The Foreign Secretary has spoken to me on this subject" is a pointer in this direction.[95]

Also, the prime minister's enthusiasm for using bombing as a punishment had led to excesses in rhetoric from time to time. These remarks occasionally required others, including Harris, to set Churchill's 'moral compass straight.' The repeated considerations of reprisal raids in response to the German razing of Lidice, Czechoslovakia in 1942, and the *Crossbow* campaign against the V-weapons in 1944, constitute proof of this trend in the PM's behaviour.[96] It should be noted that Churchill was inconsistent in his pugnaciousness with respect to bombing policy throughout the course of the war, but particularly towards the end of European hostilities, when he was undoubtedly considering both his legacy and his political future. For example, detractors of the campaign have made much of his "Are we beasts?" remarks at Chequers on the night of 27 June 1943, after viewing a film showing the bombing of German centres. Both Churchill and Sir Arthur Harris were prone to excesses of rhetoric on occasion. It was, quite simply, part and parcel of the flamboyant nature of these exceptional wartime leaders.

Portal enthusiastically endorsed Harris's views, specifically, with respect to the Dresden raids, and generally, with respect to area bombing. And the Prime Minister's Minute had so shocked the Chiefs of Staff that Portal, backed wholeheartedly by Sir Archibald Sinclair, asked Churchill to withdraw it.

CREDIT: LAC PL32218.

The *Luftwaffe* base at Volkel, Holland, after a particularly successful Bomber Command attack.

In fairness, Churchill recognized the validity of the arguments and concerns of his Chiefs, and on 1 April 1945, he approved the substitution of a considerably more guarded and restrained note. What follows is the formal request for removal of the offending first Minute and presentation of the replacement correspondence.

D.89/5

TOP SECRET

OFFICE OF THE MINISTER OF DEFENCE
PRIME MINISTER

After yesterday's Staff Conference, you said you would withdraw your "rough" minute, No.D.83/5 of 28th March, to the Chiefs of Staff Committee and C.A.S. about the bombing of German cities, and you instructed me to re-draft the minute in less rough terms.

I.   A redraft is submitted herewith for your conside-
     ration.

II. Meanwhile all copies of your previous minute are
     being withdrawn.

~H.L. Ismay
30 March 1945 [97]

TOP SECRET

PRIME MINISTER'S

PERSONAL MINUTE

Serial No. D.89/5

GENERAL ISMAY FOR C.O.S. COMMITTEE
C.A.S.

It seems to me that the moment has come when the ques-tion of the so-called "area bombing" of German cities should be reviewed from the point of view of our own interests. If we come into control of an entirely ruined land, there will be a great shortage of accommodation for ourselves and our Allies: and we shall be unable to get housing materials out of Germany for our own needs because some temporary provision would have to be made for the Germans themselves. We must see to it that our attacks do not do more harm to ourselves in the long run than they do to the enemy's immediate war effort. Pray let me have your views.

W.S.C.

28.3.45[98]

The revised Minute contained no reference to either "terror" attacks, or, specifically, to the raid on Dresden. Nevertheless, the damage had already been done, and in spite of Lord Ismay's assurances to the contrary, the first Minute also remained on file, and the effects of public scrutiny and analysis of it in future would be far-reaching.

With a View to the Future

CREDIT: IWM TR2858

Sir Winston Churchill and his Combined Chiefs of Staff, 1945, Sir Charles (later Viscount) Portal, Sir Alan Brooke, and Sir Andrew Cunningham.

As spring 1945 continued to unfold, the prime minister's newfound determination to put an end to the bombing of the German cities took effect rapidly. The fundamental guidance implied in the revised 1 April Minute had been acted upon promptly by the Air Staff. That same day, Sir Charles Portal recommended the termination of the area bombing offensive, other than that portion needed to support the land and sea campaigns. The Air Staff recommendations were subsequently approved up the chain of command, and Sir Arthur Harris was so informed on 6 April.[99] However, Portal very clearly articulated the purpose *of*, the justification *of*, and the caveats *under which* area bombing could still be conducted, if necessary. Portal has been cited frequently, like Churchill, as having an eye to the historical record and to distancing himself from Harris and from Bomber Command's campaign against the industrialized cities. However, in spite of the aforementioned disagreements with Harris, Portal staunchly defended Harris to those in higher authority, and he made it very clear that area bombing still had its place. He remained convinced that it was useful under certain circumstances, even at that late stage of the war. He also made it clear that the Command's precision attack capability was relatively newfound, and that, even with all the technological and tactical advances, it had its limitations, and precision bombing capabilities were still not widely practiced by the bulk of the Main Force. Portal's document to the Prime Minister's Office (PMO) and to the Combined Joint Chiefs of Staff outlining these considerations is therefore heavily excerpted here:

TOP SECRET

AREA BOMBING

Note by Chief of the Air Staff

- It is only in recent months that the development of night fighting technique has enabled us success-
-fully to undertake the night attack of particular industrial plants or relatively small objectives. By day, the successful bombing of these objectives requires clear skies over the target, conditions which occur on few occasions in the year. For these and other reasons, it has been an essential part of our policy, in order to extract from our bomber

forces the maximum continuity and weight of attack of which they are capable, to attack important concentrations of German war industry by means of area attack.

- The objects of attacking industrial areas have been:

    (a) To destroy important industrial plants and to disorganize essential services and labour.

    (b) To disrupt communications vital to the maintenance of order and the smooth and efficient working of the military supply organization to the areas immediately behind the enemy's fighting fronts.

    (c) To disorganize and disrupt the Nazi organization.

    (d) To force the enemy to employ in defence, repair and rehabilitation measures, resources and manpower which would otherwise be used both in war production and in strengthening the offensive power of his armed forces.

- In spite of recent advances in our ability to make precise attacks at night, the operational considerations which have in the past necessitated area attacks still exist. Nevertheless, it is recognized that at this advanced stage of the war no great or immediate additional advantage can be expected from the attack of the remaining industrial centres of Germany, because it is improbable that the full effects of further area attacks upon the enemy's war industries will have time to mature before hostilities cease…

- There may still be occasions, however, when the disintegration of enemy resistance can best be brought about through the medium of area bombing. These may arise in the following circumstances.

    (a) If resistance should stiffen on the Western Front or fail to disintegrate on the Eastern

Front, attacks on built-up areas immediately behind the fronts holding reserves and maintenance organizations, and engaged in handling military supplies, may be as effective in the preparation for an assault as they have proved in the past…

(b) It may become a military requirement to attack the communication systems of Central and Southern Germany, over which the enemy may attempt to move forces between the two fronts, or to withdraw to the redoubt in Southern Germany. The time factor may not always allow us to await precise bombing conditions and area bombing will then prove a necessity.

(c) There is strong evidence that the German High Command, its attendant staffs and Government Departments and the Party Organization are to be established in a number of Thuringian towns for the purpose of directing continued resistance. The destruction of these towns by means of area attack may then become a military requirement.

(d) The German Navy has been forced by territorial losses to withdraw from the Eastern Baltic and to concentrate in the Western Baltic and North Sea ports, especially at Kiel … The attack of this target, which is already ordered, may well involve widespread devastation in the town of Kiel with results which will approximate those of an area attack.

• We appreciate the importance of refraining from the unnecessary destruction of towns and facilities which will be needed by our own troops or for Allied reconstruction purposes. If, however, we were to restrict our bomber forces to visual precision attack we should certainly reduce the contribution which they can make towards hastening the collapse of the enemy. It is considered that area attacks are still justified strategically, insofar as they are calculated to assist in the advance of

the Allied armies into Germany or in shortening the
period of the war.[100]

In short order, Washington was advised of the intended British change
in direction of strategic bombing policy, an initiative that the Americans soon fully endorsed and embraced in Europe.[101] Shortly thereafter,
hostilities in Europe would conclude, but a vast amount of unfinished
business still remained in the Pacific theatre. Strategic bombing had
truly come of age in the European theatre of operations, and many of
the bloody lessons learned there would soon be applied to telling effect
against the Empire of the Sun.

CREDIT: USAF Museum 090625-F-1234K-298.

Boeing B-29 *Superfortresses* inbound to a Japanese target, 1945.

Area Bombing and the Japanese War

Not the least of the wartime contributions of the Allied bombing campaign in Europe was its influence upon the war against the Japanese

empire. In the Pacific theatre, B-29 *Superfortresses* of the US Twenti-
eth Air Force started pounding the Japanese home islands from bases in the Marianas in late 1944. However, their attempt at precision
bombing from high level using high explosive weaponry proved
relatively ineffective. Early in March 1945, they borrowed a page from
the area bombing methods honed in Europe, abandoned attempts at
precision bombardment, and switched their bomb runs to delivery
from medium level against area targets, commencing with incendiary laydowns. The high water mark of these raids was that conducted
against Tokyo on 9/10 March 1945, which left nearly 125,000 killed
and over a million homeless.[102] Overall, by war's end, nearly 44 percent
of 63 major Japanese cities had been laid to waste, and 42 percent of
the nation's industrial capacity had been destroyed.[103] Intensely de-
moralizing, these raids brought Japan to the brink of surrender. And
yet, based upon the fierce determination to resist an Allied invasion of
the home islands, exemplified by the sacrifice of 2530 Japanese Navy
aircrew members[104] and at least as many Army aircrew[105] on *Kamikaze*
missions directed against Allied shipping, the last of which took
place on the day of cessation of hostilities, 15 August 1945, not to
mention the highly significant losses incurred in late-war land battles,
particularly at Iwo Jima and Okinawa, the Allied Executive was gravely
concerned about the blood costs to *both* sides should an invasion of
the home islands prove necessary. Winston Churchill elaborates:

> We had contemplated the desperate resistance of the Japanese
> fighting to the death with Samurai devotion, not only in
> pitched battles, but in every cave and dugout... To quell the
> Japanese resistance man by man and to conquer the country
> yard by yard might well require the loss of a million American
> lives and half that number of British – or more if we could get
> them there: for we were resolved to share the agony.[106]

By the summer of 1945, extensive planning was taking place for
Operation *Downfall*, just such an invasion, and on a scale dwarfing

that accomplished on D-Day, scheduled for commencement on 1 November 1945, initially through the southernmost island of Kyushu. Recent and compelling research makes the point that Churchill's 'blood cost' estimate was actually rather conservative, and the true estimates Allied planning forces were working with at the time predicted 1.7 to 4 million casualties[107] Indeed, the Supreme War Council, now under the control of Prime Minister Admiral Suzuki Kantaro, who had, in turn, replaced General Tojo Hideki and General Koiso Kuniaki in the position, was determined to commit the Japanese people to mass suicide if necessary, calling "...for the sacrifice of up to 100,000,000 Japanese lives, if necessary, to repel the Allied invasion of the home islands."[108] The area bombing of Japan had certainly dealt a debilitating blow to the Japanese war industries, and the remaining factories were on the verge of collapsing for wont of component parts and damage to infrastructure. And yet, in July 1945, the Japanese aviation industry was still capable of producing over 1000 military aircraft per month, and 12,700 aircraft and 18,600 pilots were still available for home defence.[109] There was also no shortage of suicidally-inspired airmen available and willing to substitute courage for technological inadequacy, and to dive their aircraft into a massed Allied invasion force. Furthermore, "...orders went out that every Japanese man between the ages of 15 and 60 and all women aged 17 to 40 would meet the invaders at beaches with sharpened bamboo poles. Allied peace feelers were rejected."[110]

CREDIT: USAF Museum 090625-F-1234K-274.

B-29s during a bomb run.

At home, all the Allied nations were becoming increasingly war weary in light of the extensive casualties and privations endured during the last calendar year of the European and Asian wars, and economies that had been excessively 'tapped' by war expenses to date. Labour unrest was intensifying, particularly in Britain. Therefore, the perceived cost of invading the home islands, both in America and in Britain, posed serious challenges to public will and support. Although it was a painful decision for the Allies, the two atomic drops on Hiroshima and Nagasaki, the epitome of strategic area bombardment, with the concomitant loss of an additional 150,000 Japanese citizens [and many more to follow from radiation poisoning], when combined with a rapidly worsening war situation, the entry of the USSR into the Pacific war, and the continued decimation of their industrial cities, all helped convince the Japanese that further resistance was pointless. Defending against massed fleets of formidable, heavily-protected B-29 *Superfortresses* was difficult enough, but the atomic drops helped convince the Japanese that they were relatively powerless to defend the entire nation from the high and fast flying, singly-penetrating B-29s that could be using atomic weapons on any part of the nation, the ultimate 'shell game,' to draw an analogy.[111]

Finally, on 10 August 1945, the Japanese stated that Imperial Japan would accept the surrender terms announced at the Potsdam Conference the month prior as long as the Allied powers explicitly allowed Emperor Hirohito to remain as the country's sovereign ruler. The Allies, in turn, "...announced their receipt of the Japanese message and accepted the stipulation regarding Emperor Hirohito's retention yet pointedly added that the divine descendant of the sun goddess Amaterasu-ō-mi-kami would be subject to Allied authority."[112] The underscoring of the futility of further resistance, plus the guaranteed preservation of the Japanese monarchy, spared the Japanese people from the obligation of being killed to the last available man and woman. Therefore, strategic bombing undoubtedly played its part in preventing many casualties, both Allied and Japanese, by helping to eliminate the need for an armed invasion of the Japanese mainland, the costs of which, measured by any yardstick, would have been horrific.

CREDIT: USAF Museum 090625-F-1234K-267.

B-29s at bomb release, as viewed from the cockpit of one of their own.

The Balance Sheet

Critics of the bomber offensive, including Randall Hansen in *Fire and Fury*, frequently suggest that the materiel and human cost of the campaign far overshadowed the gains, and that the resources dedicated to it could have been more effectively utilized elsewhere. They have argued that the combat manpower could have been better used in the other fighting services, especially by the army during the grueling campaign in Northwest Europe, and industry could have been used to produce more weapons for these fighting services. However, proponents of this line assume that the weight of effort expended upon the bombing campaign was inordinately high. Richard Overy maintains that it was actually rather modest. "Measured against the totals for the entire war effort (production and fighting), bombing absorbed 7 percent, rising to 12 percent in 1944-45. Since at least a proportion of bomber production went to other theatres of war [and to other Commands – D.B.], the aggregate figures for the direct bombing of Germany were certainly smaller than this. Seven percent of Britain's war effort can hardly be regarded as an unreasonable allocation of resources."[113] Further, although some significant infantry shortages were experienced in 1944, those shortages never reached an extremely critical overall level and they were eventually rectified. With respect to materiel, none of the services was conspicuously wanting for anything by 1943, and the British effort was thereafter bolstered by substantial North American war production.

CREDIT: USA⁼ Museum 060517-F-12345-003.

A B-17 *Flying Fortress* disintegrates in mid-air from battle damage.

Much of the criticism of the bombing campaign has focused upon the human cost, the unquestionably heavy loss rates endured by Anglo-American aircrews, 81,000 of whom forfeited their lives aboard 18,000 downed aircraft from the Eighth Air Force and Bomber Command alone. On the Axis side, approximately 593,000 non-combatant fatalities are attributable to the bombings. However, these losses need to be placed in perspective, especially when compared to the 20-27 million war dead suffered by the Soviet Union and the millions exterminated by the Nazis. Nonetheless, the human cost of the campaign was formidable.

During the war, Bomber Command's 125,000 airmen flew 364,514 sorties over Europe, and the majority of the tonnage was dropped from the summer of 1944 until the cessation of hostilities. Approximately 74 percent of the total tonnage was delivered after 1 January 1944, and 70 percent of the total after 1 July 1944, from which time forward the Bomber Command loss rates were greatly reduced. "If the bombing of Germany had little effect on production prior to July 1944, it is not only because she had idle resources upon which to draw, but because the major weight of the air offensive against her had not been brought to bear. After the air war against Germany was launched on its full scale, the effect was immediate."[114]

The damage meted out to the industrial centres was horrific.

CREDIT: LAC PL42518.

DAVID L. BASHOW

The Contributions to Victory of the Bomber Offensive

The gains were not only those directly attributable to the bombing, such as the actual destruction of targets, but they also constituted a host of indirect benefits brought on as adjuncts to the bombing. In Richard Overy's words:

> From [renowned economist John Kenneth] Galbraith onwards the view has taken root that the only thing that Bomber Command did, or was ordered to do, was to attack German cities with indifferent accuracy. The Bombing Surveys devoted much of their effort to measuring the direct physical damage to war production through city bombing. This has produced since the war a narrow economic interpretation of the bombing offensive that distorts both the purposes and nature of Britain's bombing effort to an extraordinary degree.[115]

While part of the bombing effort was to be directed at Germany's home front military and economic structures, very large portions of the overall effort were directed at many other targets for which the Command's aircraft were needed. Again, as Overy mentions, not even half the Command's total wartime dropped bomb tonnage was dedicated to the industrial cities.[116] Also, during the latter stages of the campaign, even attacks against industrialized cities were frequently tactical rather than strategic, conducted in support of the advancing Allied land armies. For much of the first four years of the war, support for naval operations, particularly the mining of enemy littoral waters and the Western Baltic Sea, and attacks against the U-Boat production and operational facilities, comprised a significant portion of the Command's overall effort,[117] while for much of 1944, it was extensively used in support of the invasion of Northwest Europe. Additionally, Command aircraft were utilized for reconnaissance, for propaganda missions, for electronic warfare and deception operations, for support to Occupied Europe's resistance movements, and, for humanitarian aid and mercy missions towards the end of hostilities. Bomber Command was a true 'Jack-of-all-trades,' and it required the full resolution of its commanders not to become excessively and repeatedly diverted from its primary mandate, due to all the competing demands upon its limited resources.

The ruined city of Cologne, including a destroyed bridge, 1945.

CREDIT: LAC PL42542.

That said, and with the benefit of '20/20 hindsight,' while Arthur Harris was undoubtedly correct in his assessment of the need for a broad application of area bombing during the early years of the campaign, his dogged rejection of the so-called 'panacea' targets later in the war appears to have been somewhat myopic. Albert Speer and others dreaded timely follow-on efforts to the highly successful 1943 attacks on the Ruhr dams, Hamburg, and the ball bearing industry, and they believed

DAVID L. BASHOW

that such a concentration of effort at the time would have been cataclysmic for the Reich.[118] Similarly, an earlier and more dedicated application of effort against the enemy's oil resources, which pitted the Commander-in-Chief Bomber Command against the Chief of the Air Staff, *might* have brought the European war to a somewhat earlier conclusion. But such is the fog of war, and Arthur Harris sincerely believed he was following the correct course and was utilizing his command to inflict the most damage under the circumstances presented to him. And the course he chose, the targets he elected to pursue, perhaps at the cost of others more viable, were certainly not without merit or justification. The wisdom of hindsight needs to be tempered with the perceptions of the day. Furthermore, Harris was firmly convinced from an early stage of the bombing campaign that frequent, concentrated repeat visits to specific targets would incur prohibitive losses to Bomber Command.

Robin Neillands believes that, unlike the later atomic drops upon Japan, Harris simply did not have the weapon to devastate Germany in a manner that would concomitantly crush the German will to resist. Furthermore, Neillands opines:

> ...[that Harris] was also hindered throughout his campaign by a classic piece of military miscalculation, a failure by the Allied Combined Chiefs of Staff to maintain the aim. The aim of Bomber Command operations, apart from the time they began in 1939, *was to carry the war to the heart of the enemy homeland.* That was what the strategic bomber was *for*, and no one in authority disputed this. "There is one thing that will bring him [Hitler] down, and that is an absolutely devastating, exterminating attack by heavy bombers on the Nazi homeland. We must be able to overwhelm him by these means, without which I do not see a way through." Thus wrote Winston Churchill in 1940... [But] what Harris needed... as more aircraft and a free hand. Instead, there was a failure, at

all levels, to maintain his intention and carry it through. The main failure lay in not providing Bomber Command with the wherewithal to carry out this declared intention; it was not the fault of Air Chief Marshal Harris. From the earliest days of the war there was a continual diversion of bomber strength, with aircraft and crews sent to North Africa and Italy, to Coastal Command and to the Far East. This steady drain prevented Harris from ever achieving the size of force he needed to carry out the instructions he was given.[119]

The bomber offensive made possible a combat initiative that was deemed vital, not just for the damage it would cause the Third Reich, but for the galvanizing of both British and global support. It certainly affected American and Commonwealth opinion, as well as that of potential allies and enslaved nations, telegraphing British resolve to forcefully press home the fight against the tyranny of Nazism, alone if necessary. Its very prosecution assured Britain a pivotal say in the conduct of the war. It also did wonders for home front morale, bolstering the British public in a time of great need for reassurance and hope. This evidence of commitment was never more important than after the German invasion of the Soviet Union during the summer of 1941. The bombing offensive constituted a second front, a significant source of relief to the beleaguered Soviets when no other offensive action was realistic or even possible. Later, bombing's contributions would become a prerequisite to the successful invasion of northwest Europe; "...an independent campaign to pave the way for a combined arms invasion of Hitler's Europe."[120] From April until September 1944, the majority of Bomber Command's activities were conducted in lockstep with the preparation, execution, and aftermath of the invasion through Normandy. And in the wake of this effort, the Command would deal decisive blows to the enemy's transportation and petroleum resources, effectively paralyzing the Third Reich in its final hours.

DAVID L. BASHOW

With respect to the charge that German war production actually increased after the start of the CBO, that is because a state of Total War was declared only after the German defeat at Stalingrad in February 1943 and production then went to a frantic '24 and 7' mode from what had been, at Hitler's direction, a relatively sedentary pace, since he was adamant that the military endeavours of the Reich would not interfere with the consumer industries. And this vast acceleration of production was borne largely on the backs of millions of slave labourers dragooned in from the occupied territories of the Reich. It is difficult to conceive of just what the Germans would have been able to accomplish, had they *not* been forced into a very demanding industrial decentralization program,[121] had they *not* been forced to honour the bombing threats through so much bolstering of their homeland defences,[122] had they maintained uninterrupted use and control of their production facilities, and had they maintained unimpeded use of their very diversified transportation networks.

CREDIT: LAC PL41055

"Oscar," a very successful *Halifax* III.

Also, contrary to the assertions of Hansen and other detractors, while Air Chief Marshal Sir Arthur Harris was undoubtedly the most determined senior *practitioner* of area bombing, he was certainly not the *architect* of it. That distinction would need to be applied to a cadre of individuals, but most importantly, to the Chief of the Air Staff Sir Charles Portal, and to the British prime minister. And it was Churchill who actually ordered the attacks on Dresden in February 1945, at the behest of the Soviet Union, which was then engaged in major offensive operations 100 miles east of the city, a reality from which Churchill, to his discredit, later attempted to distance himself.

The Morality Issue

Readers also need to bear in mind that bombing conducted for the purpose of lowering enemy morale was not the exclusive purview of Bomber Command. Earlier, we mentioned American attitudes and policies with respect to area bombing. Major General Frederick L. Anderson Jr. was the commanding general of the American Eighth Bomber Command within the parent Eighth Air Force for most of the combined portion of the European air war. With respect to the isolated, late-war American bombing of mainly smaller urban centres, General Anderson noted that while such operations were not expected in themselves to shorten the war, "...it is expected that the fact that Germany was struck all over will be passed on, from father to son, thence to grandson, (and) that a deterrent for the initiation of future wars will definitely result."[123] In an extension of this argument, British author Keith Lowe, in his highly acclaimed 2007 release entitled *Inferno: The Destruction of Hamburg, 1943*, maintains, along with others, that the experience of this specific bombing, and the subsequent campaign against the German cities, eventually knocked militarism out of the German people.[124] Current German attitudes with respect to participation in foreign military operations certainly reinforce this point.

As the late-war evidence of Nazi atrocities mounted, there developed a significant Allied hardening of sentiment to bring the German people so completely to their knees that they would never again contemplate bringing another holocaust down upon the world. This was reflected in the partial tactical use of strategic bombers during the push through Germany in the closing weeks. If a German urban area resisted and generated Anglo-American casualties resulting from house-to-house fighting, such as had occurred at Ortona, Italy, and elsewhere in the advance across northwest Europe, it was normally shelled and bombed into rubble. However, those centres that acquiesced peacefully were normally spared further destruction. For the most part, similar courtesies were not extended during the Soviet advance, and German citizens were quite aware of the distinction being exercised by the Western Allies. These actions served to reinforce the point that no citizen of the Third Reich was immune *to* or exempt *from* the bombing, and that further armed resistance was futile. The deliberate demoralization of the enemy undoubtedly helped shatter the German will to resist, hastening the capitulation of German forces in the western urban centres, and thereby saving many lives, both Allied and Axis.

CREDIT: LAC PL42536.

Another view of Cologne in ruins, 1945.

As Richard Overy has recently postulated, perhaps the most important point to take from study of the moral argument for the bombing
campaign is *why* the two major participating democracies ultimately
"...[engaged] in forms of total war that abandoned altogether the
moral high ground they had tried to occupy in the 1930s."[125] The
British, who were the first of the two 'great democracies' to abandon
that moral high ground, were also the first to engage the Axis forces,
and they had been provided with many prior examples of indiscriminate area bombing by Germany, including Warsaw in 1939, Rotterdam,
London, and many other British cities in 1940, then Belgrade, Yugo-
slavia, and additional British urban centres in 1941 and 1942. Area
bombing was really the only viable offensive tool available to the
British at the time, and it served due notice to friends and foes alike
that Britain *could*, and *would*, fight back. It provided offensive relief
to the Soviets when no other form of concentrated, sustained attack upon
the enemy was yet possible. Further, while the premises upon which the
bombing was conducted, along with some elements of its execution,
may, in hindsight, appear somewhat flawed, substantial and repeated
feedback from intelligence sources inside the Third Reich, as referenced
herein, indicated that the bombing was scoring telling blows. Much of
this rationale was still applicable after the United States entered the
war. Further, the Americans were exerting pressure upon their British
partners to conclude the European war as expeditiously as possible, and
then to turn their combined attentions against the Japanese. The Americans also learned both through associations with the British and from
their own combat experiences, that their own bombing forces were also,
in reality, 'blunt instruments of destruction,' with little true precision
bombing capabilities. This, in spite of the long-fostered, mythological
public stance that they could deliver munitions precisely and effectively in all weather conditions. Much of the present-day abhorrence of the
wartime area bombing strategy has been fuelled by the current propensity for viewing the campaign through the lens of *today's* technological
capabilities. While existing 'smart' weapons can surgically demolish a
specific room in a building without figuratively 'rattling the china' in

an adjacent room, such technology, taken for granted today, simply was not available during the Second World War.

Readers also need to understand that, with respect to the pious post-war posturing of the Soviets concerning the bombings, Dresden and other eastern German cities were bombed to assist the Soviets in their own combat operations. Once the war was over and Dresden had fallen behind the Iron Curtain, it was not to their advantage to trumpet this bombing request to the new world order, since the ideological polarities that characterized the subsequent Cold War had already hardened.

Today, along with Randall Hansen, Margaret MacMillan, and Robert Bothwell, there are others who continue to condemn the bombing. One of the most prominent recent examples is the British philosopher Anthony C. Grayling, who has implied a 'moral equivalency' between the Allied strategic bombing campaign and the 9/11 attacks on the United States. Part of the problem, this writer believes, is a widespread current propensity to view historical decisions and the actions that resulted from them through the filtering lens of present day sensitivities and technological capabilities. History can only be judged properly from within the context of the times during which it occurred. Hindsight invariably benefits from 20/20 clarity.

As to the frequently advanced argument, fatuous at best, that the Second World War was 'Hitler's war,' and that 78 million Germans wanted no part of it, those attitudes were not much in evidence when Nazi legions were having their way with most of Eurasia during the first three years of the war. Nor is that argument of any consolation to the ghosts of the millions who were systematically exterminated in the death camps and elsewhere. Lost in much of the debate is the fact that Nazism was a thoroughly repulsive and evil force bent upon world domination. Public opinion surveys from the war confirm widespread support for the bombing. Neither politicians nor historians of the period challenged the policy extensively at the time, and while British authorities maintained staunchly that civilian casualties were nothing but "... an unfortunate by-product of attacks on industrial areas, there is little reason to believe that the general public would have complained had it been otherwise."[126] Further, there was very little questioning of the morality of the bombing during the war, and what little that did occur came primarily from isolated British religious leaders.[127]

The Legal Issue

Although the Red Cross Convention on the Protection of Civilians in Wartime was agreed upon in Stockholm in August 1948, it was never formally ratified, and the matter has only been fully codified since 1977 in the wake of the Vietnam War, when the First Protocol to the Fourth Convention expressly forbade deliberate military attacks upon civilians. And it should be emphasized that this particular legislation was made possible largely by significant technological advances with respect to weapons delivery, which have, for the most part, rendered area bombing unnecessary.

It's over. Canadian aircrew VE-Day celebrations, 8 May 1945.

CREDIT: LAC PL44007.

DAVID L. BASHOW

A Few Closing Thoughts

Bomber Command played an essential part as a guarantor of Allied victory during the Second World War. It provided an offensive tool that took the fight to the enemy when none other was available, and it gave the citizens of the Allied nations hope and pride while it did so. It provided Britain and the Dominions, through its very prosecution, a political dimension by which it could influence the conduct of the war. It demanded a significant diversion of German resources away from the Eastern Front, thereby aiding the USSR in its part of the combined struggle. It struck substantial and unrelenting blows against enemy morale. It threw Germany's broader war strategy into disarray, forcing it to adopt a *reactive* rather than a *proactive* stance though industrial decentralization, which placed unsupportable burdens on a transportation network that was already stretched to the limit. It delivered crippling blows to the enemy's sophisticated and diverse transportation network, and it generated a loss of German air superiority, along with doing much significant damage to the Reich's war industrial base. It eventually starved the nation of petroleum products, and it made the way safer for an Allied re-entry into northwest Europe in 1944. It effectively stymied German economic mobilization and technological development in many areas, and it goaded the Nazis into costly and ineffective retaliation campaigns. While a great human price was paid for these accomplishments on both the combatant sides, in relative terms, the losses incurred to the Anglo-Americans were small when compared to those suffered elsewhere, such as in the USSR. And the overall cost was relatively low as a percentage of the total war effort, considering the gains that were realized.

NOTES

1   Edward Jablonski, *America in the Air War* (Alexandria, VA: Time-Life Books, 1982), p. 142. Drawn from Wesley F. Craven and James L. Cate (eds.), *The Army Air Forces in World War II*, Vol. 7, (Chicago: University of Chicago Press, 1958).

2   Nigel Smith & Peter Hart, *Tumult in the Clouds* (London: Hodder and Stoughton, 1997), pp. 262-284.

3   John Terraine, *The Right of the Line – The Royal Air Force in the European War 1939-1945* (London: Hodder and Stoughton, 1985), p. 11.

4   Brereton Greenhous, Stephen J. Harris, William C. Johnston, and William G.P. Rawling, *The Crucible of War 1939-1945 – The Official History of the Royal Canadian Air Force – Volume III* (Toronto: University of Toronto Press, 1994), p. 528.

5   Richard Overy, *Bomber Command 1939-1945 ~ Reaping the Whirlwind* (London: HarperCollins, 1997), p. 16.

6   Greenhous *et al*, p. 535.

7   Ibid.

8   Portal to Newall, Ibid., p. 536.

9   Ibid., p. 544.

10   Special Distribution and War Cabinet Report from Switzerland, Memo No. 529, 28 July 1940, in Public Record Office (PRO) Premier 3/11/1, p. 35.

11   Sir Charles Webster and Noble Frankland, *The Strategic Air Offensive against Germany*, Vol. 1(London: Her Majesty's Stationary Office, 1961), p. 233.

12   AHB(Air Historical Branch)/II/117/1(B), p.122.

13   Sir Martin Gilbert, *Finest Hour – Winston Churchill 1939-41* (London: Heinemann, 1983), pp. 655-656.

14   Roy Conyers Nesbit, *The Battle of Britain* (Thrupp, UK: Sutton Publishing, 2000), p. 217.

15   Lord Portal, as quoted in Greenhous *et al.*, p. 539.

16   Air Ministry Guidance to Sir Richard Peirse, 25 Oct 1940, PRO Air 9/132, as quoted in Ibid.

17   Sinclair to Churchill, 7 Oct 1940, in PRO Premier 3/11/11A, p. 515.

18   Terraine, p. 276.

19   Ibid.

20   Greenhous *et al.*, p. 544.

21   Cited in various Bomber Command sources, as referenced by Greenhous *et al.*, p. 550.

22   Frederick Lindemann (Lord Cherwell) was a scientist and academic, and a true *eminence grise* as Churchill's great friend. But his influence often extended beyond his expertise, and he was not a military man. "Cherwell also used his position to promote particular strategies and tactics, even if it meant distorting the scientific evidence." David Zimmerman, *Britain's Shield – Radar and the Defeat of the Luftwaffe* (Stroud, UK: Sutton, 2001), p. 231. For more specifics, see Richard Holmes, *Battlefields of the Second World War* (London: BBC Worldwide, 2001), p. 183.

23   Henry Probert, *Bomber Harris – His Life and Times* (Toronto: Stoddart, 2001), p. 139.

24   Charles Webster and Noble Frankland, *The Strategic Air Offensive against Germany*, Vol. 4, Appendix 8 (London: Her Majesty's Stationary Service, 1965), p. 144.

25   Air Historical Branch (AHB) Bomber Command Narrative, IV, p. 130, DHist (Canada) File 86/286; Bottomly to Baldwin, 14 Feb 1942, quoted in Webster and Frankland, SAO, Vol. 4, Appendix 8, pp. 143-145. Portal to Bottomly, 15 Feb 1942, quoted in Webster and Frankland, SAO, Vol. 1, p. 324, all in Greenhous *et al.*, p. 576.

26   Williamson Murray, *Strategy for Defeat – The Luftwaffe 1933-1945* (Secaucus, NJ: 1986) p. 105.

27   <http://www.nucleus.com/twright/bc-stats/html/>, accessed 15 May 2005. Richard Overy's research closely mirrors these findings and acknowledges the diversified effort in many other areas. "Between February 1942, when Air Marshal Arthur Harris became Commander-in-Chief, and May 1945, some 43 percent of Bomber Command tonnage was directed at industrial centres in Germany, while over 40 percent was devoted to support for land operations, long range reconnaissance, mining, supporting resistance operations, attacks on communications and airfields, and the war at sea." Overy, p. 51. Other command taskings included designated precision attacks, propaganda (leaflet) raids, electronic warfare support, and humanitarian relief missions towards the end of hostilities. David Bashow, *No Prouder Place ~ Canadians and the Bomber Command Experience 1939-1945* (St. Catharines, ON: Vanwell Publishing, 2005), p. 459.

28   Overy, p. 80.

29   Martin Middlebrook, "Bomber Command's War ~ The Turning Points-Part 2," in *Flypast*, No. 206, 1995.

30   Churchill to Sinclair, 13 Mar 1942, Portal Papers, Folder 3, in Probert, p. 133.

31   John Singleton, "Report on the Bombing of Germany to Prime Minister Churchill," 20 May 1942, in PRO Premier 3/11/4, p. 124.

32   Air Intelligence Result of Recent RAF Attacks Report to Prime Minister, 23 Sept 1942, in PRO Premier 3/11/12, p. 621.

33   Air Intelligence Report No. 346 to CAS, 22.9.42, in PRO Premier 3/11/12, pp. 627-629.

34   Winston Churchill, policy note to War Cabinet, 16 Dec 1942, in PRO Premier 3/11/6, pp. 179-182.

35   Edward Jablonski, *America in the Air War* (Alexandria, VA: Time-Life Books, 1982), p. 56.

36   Ibid.

37   Webster and Frankland, *Strategic Air Offensive*, Vol. 4, Appendix 8, Directive xxviii, pp. 153-154.

38   Overy, p. 111.

39   *Pointblank* Directive, 10 June 1943, in Webster and Frankland, Strategic Air Offensive, Vol. 1, pp. 158-160.

40   Ibid., p. 2.

41   In the wake of the Hamburg raids, Albert Speer made a statement to Hitler that certainly got the attention of Harris and his planners, namely, that if six more German cities were pummeled as badly as had been Hamburg, Germany might not be able to continue the war. Quoted in Martin Middlebrook, "Bomber Command ~ Part Three," in *Flypast*, No. 207 (October 1998), p. 50.

42   Quoted in Webster and Frankland, *Strategic Bomber Offensive*, Vol. 2, (London: Her Majesty's Stationary Service, 1963), p. 190.

43   Webster and Frankland, *Strategic Bomber Offensive*, Vol. 4, p. 172.

44   Terraine, p. 673.

45   Probert, p. 306.

46   Ibid., p. 305.

47   Ibid., p. 7.

48   Various official British and American sources, including W.F. Craven and J.L. Cate, *The Army Air Forces in World War II* (Chicago: University of Chicago Press, 1958), Vol. 3, p. 670.

49   Webster and Frankland, *The Strategic Bomber Offensive*, Vol. 3, pp. 81-94.

50   During the four effective months of European combat in 1945, Bomber Command would drop 181,000 tons of bombs, which constituted nearly one-fifth of the aggregate for the entire war. Considering the multiplicity of "diversions" placed upon the command, even at this late stage of the war, and that 66,482 tons (36.6 percent of the effort) was devoted to attacks on the cities, it is commendable that a full 47,510 tons or 26.2 percent of the total effort for the period was devoted to oil targets. Terraine, pp. 678-679.

51   Probert, p. 312.

52   Ibid., p. 292.

53   During the two months of the Transportation Plan's implementation, more than 42,000 tons were dropped by Bomber Command on 33 of the 37 assigned railway centres. During the same period, USAAF forces delivered 11,648 tons on 23 of their assigned targets. John D.R. Rawlings, *The History of the Royal Air Force* (Feltham, Middlesex, UK: Temple Press, 1984), p. 146.

54   Franklin D'Olier *et al.*, *The US Strategic Bomb Survey – Overall Report – European War – September 30, 1945* (Washington: US Government Printing Office, 1945), p. 62.

55   Sir Charles Portal, Memorandum for British Chiefs of Staff, 3 Nov 1942, in PRO Air 14/739A.

56   Terraine, p. 537, and Overy, p. 209.

57   Martin Middlebrook, "Bomber Command – The Turning Points," in *Flypast*, No. 209, [December 1996], p. 85; Ancillary data from Murray, p. 178; and Terraine, pp. 678-679.

58   Neillands, p. 340; Bomber Command Diary (online), at <http://www.raf.mod.uk/bombercommand/diary/diary 1944_1.html>, p. 7, accessed 14 January 2008.

59   Brereton Greenhous and Hugh A. Halliday, *Canada's Air Forces 1914-1999* (Montreal: Art Global, 1999), p. 118.

60   Bomber Command Diary, October 1944, p. 1.

61   Neillands, p. 337.

62   Ibid.

63   David R. Mets, *Master of Airpower: General Carl A. Spaatz* (Novato, CA: Presidio Press, 1997), p. 269.

64   Neillands, p. 341.

65   Paul Addison and Jeremy A. Crang, *Firestorm* (London: Pimlico, 2006), p. 102.

66   303rd BG [H] Combat Mission No. 311, 3 February 1945, at <http://www.303rdbg.com/missionreports/311.pdf>, accessed 10 March 2008.

67   *Bombing of Berlin in World War II*, at <http://en.wikipedia.org/wiki/Bombing_of_Berlin_in_World_War_II>, accessed 10 March 2008, and Frederick Taylor, *Dresden – Tuesday, February 13, 1945* (New York: HarperCollins, 2004), p. 354.

68   Neillands, p. 370.

69   Craven and Cate, *The Army Air Forces in World War II*, Vol. 3, p. 6.

70   Richard Overy, *Are We Beasts?* A review of *The Fire: The Bombing of Germany 1940-1945*, by Jörg Friedrich, and *Inferno: The destruction of Hamburg*, by Keith Lowe, in Literary Review, March 2007, at <http://www.literaryreview.co.uk/overy_03_07.html>, accessed 7 March 2008.

71   Richard G. Davis, "German Railroads and Cities: US Bombing Policy, 1944-1945, in *Air Power History*, Vol. 42, No. 2 (Summer 1995), from Tami Davis Biddle, "Dresden 1945: Reality, History, and Memory," in *Project Muse – Scholarly Journals Online of The Journal of Military History*, (Lexington, VA: Virginia Military Institute, April 2008), pp. 433, Note 62.

72   Joel Punches, *B-17F Flight Log (5 Sept 1943-21 Feb 1944)*, accessed 15 January 2011.

73   Neillands, p. 339

74   Bill Swetman, "Avro Lancaster," in Jeffrey L. Ethell (ed.) *The Great Book of World War II Airplanes* (Tokyo: Zokeisha Publications, 1984), pp. 417-418.

75   Neillands, p. 255.

76   Ibid., p. 293.

77   This assumes that the lead bombardier 'got it right' in the first instance. Reaction times would further increase bomb impact dispersion, as would the normal spread formation of a bombing squadron. *Major Deceptions on Contrails Unmasked*, at <http://goodsky.homestead.com/files/deception5.html>, accessed 12 March 2008. Of note, of the 39 B-17s of the 303rd Bomb Group that bombed Berlin on 3 February 1945, 23 were crewed by togglers versus bombardiers. <http://www.303rdbg.com/missionreports/311.pdf>, accessed 10 March 2008.

78   Group Captain Peter W. Gray, "Dresden 1945 – Just another Raid?" *Royal Air Force Airpower Review*, Vol. 4, No. 1 (Spring 2001), p. 5.

79   Quoted in Webster and Frankland, *Strategic Bomber Offensive*, Vol. 3, p. 101.

80   Sinclair to Churchill (Top Secret), 26 January 1945, in PRO Premier 3/12, p. 37.

81   Prime Minister's Personal Minute to Sinclair, 26 January 1945, in PRO Premier 3/12, p. 34.

82   Sinclair to Churchill (Top Secret), 27 January 1945, in PRO Premier 3/12, p. 33.

83   Gray, "Dresden, 1945," p. 6.

84   Ibid.

85   Biddle, p. 428, Note 45.

86   Probert, p. 320, and Gray, p. 8.

87   For a more detailed discussion on the Dresden raids, including the justification and the results, see David L. Bashow, *None but the Brave* (Kingston, ON: CDA Press, 2009), pp. 151-153, and Notes 85-88.

88   *Der Spiegel* Online International, 10 February 2008, Frederick Taylor, "How Many Died in the Bombing of Dresden?" at <http://www.spiegel.de/international/germany/0,1518,581992,00.html>, and *Der Spiegel* Online International, 13 February 2009, Frederick Taylor/ *Der Spiegel* interview, "The Logic behind the Destruction of Dresden," at <http://www.spiegel.de/international/germany/0,1518,607524,00.html>.

89   Quoted in Webster and Frankland, *Strategic Air Offensive*, Vol. 3, p. 112.

90   Neillands, p. 373.

91   Minute (Top Secret) Churchill to Ismay *et al*, 28 March 1945, at PRO Premier 3/12, p. 23.

92   Gray, "Dresden 1945," p. 9.

93   Quoted in Probert, p. 322. The paraphrased remark of Bismarck's, made at the Congress of Berlin in 1878, reads as follows: "The whole of the Balkans is not worth the bones of a single Pomeranian grenadier."

94   Bomber Command Official History, Vol. III, pp. 117-119, Folder H84, dated 18 and 21 April 1945, in Probert, p. 326.

95   Neillands, p. 372.

96   The first case involves entreaties from Eduard Beneš, the exiled President of Czechoslovakia, to Churchill following the razing of Lidice in the wake of the Reinhard Heydrich assassination on 29 May 1942. Examined in Bashow, *No Prouder Place*, pp. 91-93, and Notes 68-72, especially Letter and Minute in PRO Premier 3/11/12, p. 667, Letter Beneš to Churchill, 15 June 1942, in PRO Premier 3/11/12, p. 669, and Letter Harris to Churchill, 15 June 1942, in PRO Premier 3/11/12, p. 666. The *Crossbow* experience involved the Prime Minister, this time asking the Chiefs of Staff to consider reprisals (bombing small German towns and use of poison gas) against the German people for the V-weapon attacks upon Britain. [Prime Minister's Minute No D. 217/4, 5 July 1944, and COS Minute to Prime Minister 1126/4, 5 July 1944, both in PRO Premier 3/12, pp. 81-83]. Poison gas issue covered in Lord Tedder's *Memoirs*, and quoted in Terraine, pp. 652-653, and R.V. Jones, letter to *Daily Telegraph*, 11 June 1981. Concerning bombing the towns, the Air Staff defused the initiative, claiming that with respect to indiscriminate bombing, "We have hitherto always maintained consistently in all public statements regarding our bombing policy that it is directed against military objectives and that any damage to civilians is incidental to our attack on the German war machine. This is a moral and legal point of great importance, both now and in the Maintenance of our position after the war, and it would be greatly weakened should we now for the first time declare that we intended deliberate attacks on the civilian population as such." Examined in Bashow, pp. 341-344, and Notes 75-78, particularly War Cabinet Conclusions, Minute 4, 3 July 1944, in PRO Premier 3/12, p. 92, and Note by Air Staff, "Crossbow – Consideration of Retaliation," in PRO Premier 3/12, pp. 85-89.

97   Minute D.89/5 (Top Secret) Ismay to Churchill, 30 March 1945, at PRO Premier 3/12, p. 23.

98   Attachment (Top Secret) to Minute D.89/5 (Top Secret) Churchill to Ismay *et al*, 01 April 1945, at PRO Premier 3/12, p. 22.

99   Probert, p. 325.

100   Note (Top Secret – undated) by Sir Charles Portal, at PRO Premier 3/12. pp. 18-21.

101   Additional correspondence contained at PRO Premier 3/12, pp. 7-17.

102   H.P. Willmott, (John Keegan [ed.]), *The Second World War in the Far East* (London: Cassell, 1999), p. 202.

103   Ibid., p. 198.

104   Statistic acquired by author from Japanese Navy *Kamikaze* memorial, naval museum, Japanese Maritime Self-Defence Force Officer Candidate School, Etajima, Japan, 16 July 2002.

105   Masatake Okumiya, Jiro Horikoshi, and Martin Caidin, *Zero* (New York: ibooks, 1956, 2002), p. 354.

106   Winston Churchill, *The Second World War*, Volume 2 (New York. Time-Life Books, 1959), p. 561.

107   D.M. Giangreco, *Hell to Pay ~ Operation Downfall and the Invasion of Japan, 1945-1947* (Annapolis, MD: Naval Institute Press, 2009), pp. xv, 92.

108   Statistic acquired by author from the Hiroshima Peace Museum, Hiroshima, Japan, 15 July 2002. The Supreme Council [War Cabinet] was apparently figuratively calling for the sacrifice of every Japanese man, woman, and child, if necessary, since the total population of Japan in 1945 was just under 72 million. However, hyperbole aside, Japanese planners anticipated 20 million Japanese casualties in repelling an Allied invasion force, and an estimated 916,828 military personnel had been deployed to Kyushu to counter the invasion threat by war's end. Giangreco, pp. 92, 93, 203 [Note 50].

109   Ibid., p. xviii, and Okumiya *et al.*, pp. 362, 378.

110   Edward Jablonski, p. 169. Peter Jennings and Todd Brewster, *The Century* (New York: Doubleday, 1998), p. 276. The Allied Potsdam Declaration of 26 July 1945 called unequivocally for the "unconditional surrender" of Japan, but on 31 July, Emperor Hirohito made it clear that the 'Imperial Regalia' of Japan (i.e., the royal throne) had to be defended at all costs. *Atomic Bombings of Hiroshima and Nagasaki*, at <http://en.wikipedia.org/wiki/Atomic_bombings_of_Hiroshima_and_Nagasaki>, p. 8, Note 20. *Kido Koichi nikki* (Tokyo: Daigaku Shuppankai, 1966), pp. 1120-1121.

111 A third atomic weapon was going to be available by mid-August, and 8-9 of them were to be available for planned battlefield *tactical* use during the invasion of Kyushu in November, along with the planned use of poison gas. Giangreco, pp. 201-202.

112 Ibid., p. 110, Note 38.

113 Overy, *Bomber Command 1939-1945...*, p. 200.

114 D'Olier *et al.*, p. 71.

115 Overy, *Bomber Command 1939-1945...*, p. 183.

116 Ibid., p. 51, and Bashow, *No Prouder Place*, p. 459.

117 For a detailed discussion, see Bashow, *None but the Brave*, pp. 144-147.

118 Albert Speer, *Inside the Third Reich* (New York: Galihad, 1970), p. 286, and Joachim Fest, *Speer – The Final Verdict* (London: Weidenfeld & Nicolson, 2001), p. 166-167.

119 Neillands, p. 301.

120 Overy, *Bomber Command 1939-1945*, p. 191.

121 For a more detailed discussion, see Bashow, *None but the Brave*, p. 131 and Note 34.

122 Discussed in depth at ibid., p. 130, pp. 138-140, and Notes 32, 51-62.

123 PRO documents, as quoted in Richard Norton Taylor's "Allied Bombers Chose 'Easy' German Targets," in *The Guardian*, Thursday 23 August 2001.

124 Keith Lowe, "Inferno: The Destruction of Hamburg," in *Literary Review*, March 2007, at <http://www.literaryreview.co.uk/overy_03_07.html>, accessed 7 March 2008.

125 Richard Overy, *Are We Beasts? A Review of The Fire: The Fire Bombing of Germany 1940-1945*, by Jörg Friedrich, at ibid., accessed 23 December 2009.

126 Greenhous *et al.*, p. 726.

127 For a detailed discussion, see Bashow, *No Prouder Place*, p. 476 and Notes 108-113.

ABOUT THE AUTHOR

Lieutenant-Colonel (ret'd) David L. Bashow, OMM, CD, has written extensively in books and periodicals on a variety of defence, foreign policy, and military history topics. He is currently Editor-in-Chief of the *Canadian Military Journal* and an Associate Professor of History at the Royal Military College of Canada. Prior to *None but the Brave*, a more generic assessment of policy development and results obtained by the bomber offensive, released by the Canadian Defence Academy Press in 2008, his most recent book was entitled *No Prouder Place ~ Canadians and the Bomber Command Experience 1939-1945*. It has received outstanding reviews and is now in its second printing.

INDEX